⊖ AN OBSERVER'S GUIDE

Beginning Watercolour

Joan Scott

FREDERICK WARNE

Published by Frederick Warne (Publishers) Ltd, London, 1981

1499.1180

Acknowledgements

Figure 1 is reproduced by courtesy of The Tate Gallery, London; Figures 2 and 4 are reproduced by courtesy of the Victoria and Albert Museum, London; Figure 3 is reproduced by courtesy of the Trustees of the British Museum, London.

ISBN 0 7232 2464 1

Printed and bound in Great Britain by William Clowes (Beccles) Ltd
Beccles and London
1499.1180

Contents

Introduction to watercolour

Watercolour is pre-eminently the medium for conveying atmospheric impressions, weather conditions, and poetic interpretations of nature. It is not a medium for plodding, or 'trying to get things right', and must be attacked spontaneously after a great deal of forethought, so that, even if taken slowly, nothing is put down that is not meant. A watercolour must not look tired and overworked when it is finished and it is better to stop too soon rather than too late.

Watercolour has always been considered as a medium in which English artists particularly excel, beginning with those painting in the eighteenth and nineteenth centuries and continuing up to the present day. However,

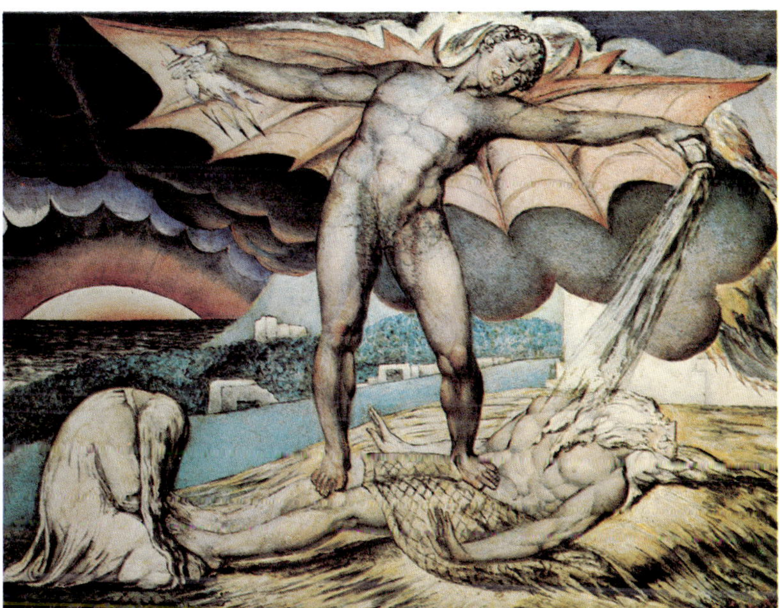

Figure 1 *Satan Smiting Job with Sore Boils* William Blake (The Tate Gallery, London)

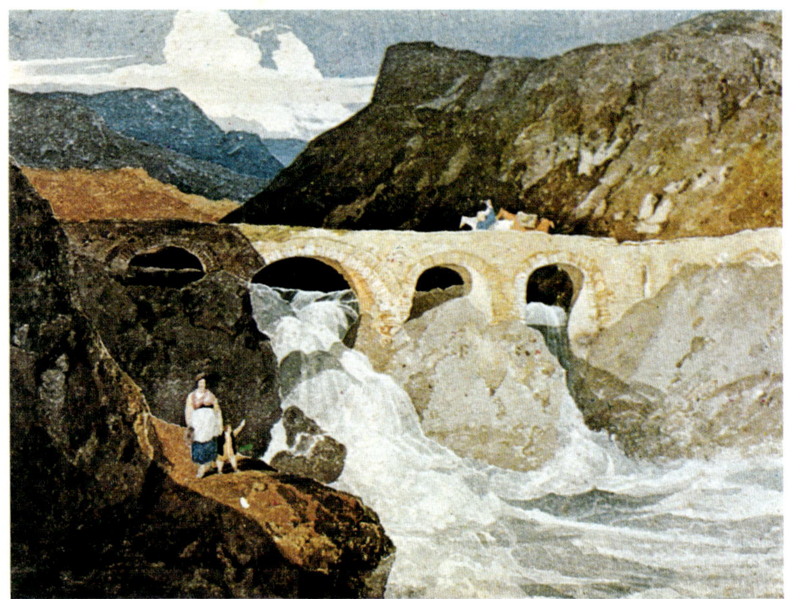

Figure 2   *Road to Capel Curig, North Wales*   John Sell Cotman (Victoria and Albert Museum, London)

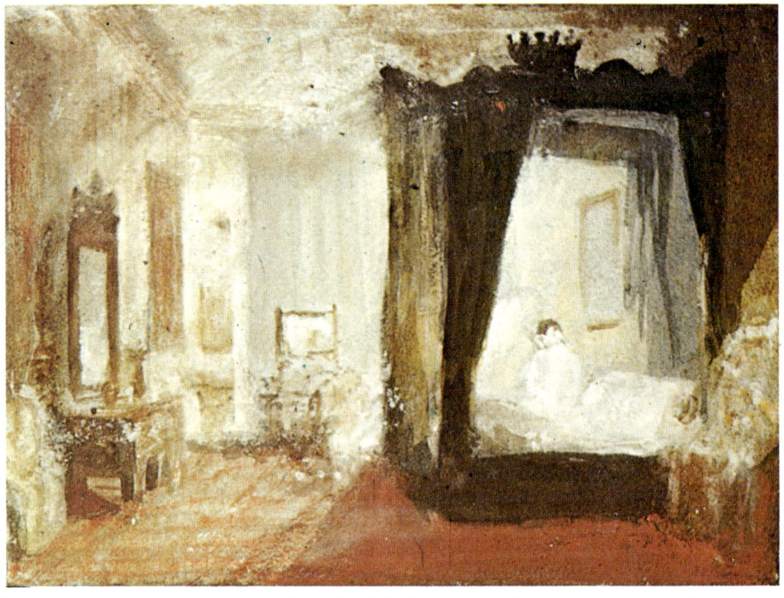

Figure 3   *Bedroom at Petworth*   J. M. W. Turner (British Museum, London)

there has been a great surge of interest and execution in this medium in America with many of the artists using it experimentally with most exciting results. Of course, watercolour was used much earlier. Dürer was using it in the fifteenth century and Bellini, Urbino and Castiglione even earlier.

Usually, watercolour is the name given to the method of painting on white, or slightly tinted, papers with transparent washes, using the white of the paper shining through the transparency to give the lights. Opaque painting is obtained by adding Chinese white to the watercolours or by using poster paint or Designer's Colours and this method of painting is called Gouache, or body colour.

Purists consider that only transparent watercolour is worthy of that name but in fact, some of the early English watercolourists like Thomas Girtin, and Turner himself, used body colour, and this can be seen in some of the lovely small sketches done on 'Turner Grey' paper.

On the whole, the early watercolourists did work with transparent washes and the Norwich School collection is particularly worth a visit. It is housed in the Castle Museum in Norwich and includes pictures by John Sell Cotman, Peter de Wint, David Cox and others.

Modern watercolourists can be seen at the annual exhibition of the Royal Society of Painters in Watercolour, held at the Mall Galleries in London, usually in the spring and this is one of the most popular exhibitions of the year.

In Figures 1, 2 and 3 will be seen samples of the work of William Blake, John Sell Cotman and James Mallord Turner, working in their individual way.

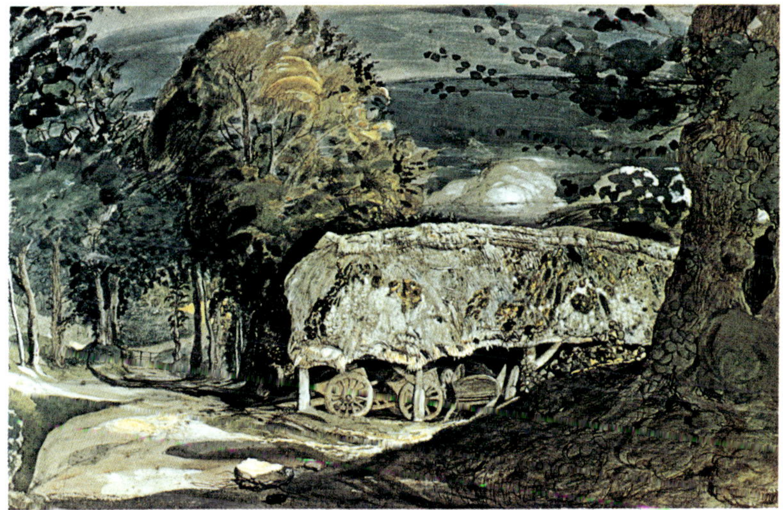

Figure 4   *Lane and Barn*   Samuel Palmer (Victoria and Albert Museum, London)

Other watercolourists using the medium more recently, within their own vision are Paul Nash, John Minton, Edward Burra, and Eric Ravilious. Of the Europeans working in watercolour, Paul Klee, August Macke and Emil Nolde were using it imaginatively in the nineteenth and early twentieth century. Figure 4 shows a picture by Samuel Palmer, who, in his 'Valley of Vision' years, has a unique place in watercolour painting. Body colour was often used, as well as sepia ink and sometimes the paintings were varnished. They are small and can be seen in the Victoria and Albert Museum, London, The Ashmolean in Oxford and The Fitzwilliam Museum in Cambridge.

For a long time, watercolour was considered as only a medium for working out a painting which would subsequently be done in oil, or used as a sketching medium. Even in our own time watercolour has been thought of as second-best, but it now seems to have come into its own again and many of the private galleries specialize in early English watercolours as well as in modern work.

Materials and equipment

Watercolours are pigment bound with gum-arabic, though according to Hilaire Hiler in *Notes on the Technique of Painting*, these days it is called gum senegal and no longer comes from Arabia. Sugar, honey and glycerine are also used in their manufacture in order to keep them moist and soft. Watercolours come in tubes, pans and cakes. Cakes are not easily come by these days but are stocked by a few Artists' Colourmen. People who have used them say that cakes are superior to tube or pan colour but I have no personal experience of them. Permanence depends upon the pigment and not upon the binder, so some colours are more permanent than others. Some will react to sulphur and other impurities in the atmosphere and some will fade if hung in a strong light for too long, which is why many of the early English watercolours in the museums are kept in folios. These can always be seen on request.

Today's Arts Materials Manufacturers (Artists' Colourmen) are experts in producing high-quality paints, and though the prices may seem high, this is because a lot of care and experiment has gone into producing the best and most permanent paints possible. It is wise to obtain a free manual from one of the manufacturers. Winsor and Newton publish one listing the composition and permanence of pigments both in watercolour and in oil. It is extremely interesting to study and I have had mine for years and still keep it handy for reference. It may be thought by beginners that permanence is not a thing that they need worry about but it is as well to begin as you mean to go on. When and if a painting is sold, or even given as a present, it is satisfactory to know that it is not going to fade or react with the atmosphere. Catalogues of artist's materials will also carry this information and will also indicate which colours are transparent. Obviously in using watercolour, which is a transparent medium, this information is a great help. Some of the less transparent colours, such as Light Red, will be necessary in the palette but the more transparent colours that are used the better.

Although for convenience we talk of pigment, some of the modern colours are synthetic dyes and although transparent and excellent colours, they will also stain the paper indelibly, which is as well to know.

Purchasing watercolours

When purchasing colours and equipment for watercolour painting, the sky is the limit, but good equipment for a beginner can be bought at a more modest cost. It pays to use the best materials when painting in this medium but the initial cost can be reduced by dispensing with some items. For instance, although a proper watercolour box fitted with tubes and pans and mixing wells is a delightful thing to have, good work can be done with a few tubes, a plastic palette with wells for mixing and a large, shallow plastic dish, as plenty of mixing area is needed; more than is usually provided in a box. What is important is an adequate brush, but more will be said about this later on.

Students often ask if tubes or pans are best to use for watercolour painting. Ideally, I think it is good to have a box with pans, and before each painting, top up each pan with a little fresh paint from a tube so that the brush is not scrubbing about in dry paint. This is very harmful to the brush and not conducive to good technique. By the time that the tube paint is used, the dry paint in the pan will be softened enough for use. Some colours do dry up in the tubes, particularly if they are not in constant use, but they can be salvaged by cutting off the bottom of the tube, opening it up, and letting the dried colour soak for a while in a little water and then placing it in a pan or using it at once. Paint that has been put out from tubes onto a palette can be kept from one session to another as, unlike oil, it can be softened with water and used until it has finally disappeared.

A beginner's palette

A suggested palette might be: Cobalt Blue, French Ultramarine, Prussian Blue, Crimson Alizarin, Light Red, Winsor or Viridian Green, Olive Green, Raw Sienna, New Gamboge, Lemon Yellow, Burnt Sienna, Burnt Umber and Payne's Grey. Other colours can be tried later but this selection is a good basic choice. Of these colours, only Light Red and Burnt Umber are not transparent in themselves, but both are useful colours. Some artists never use a bought green and always mix their own, but Winsor or Viridian Green is necessary as a base for some colours; it is advisable never to use it on its own and always use it with discretion. Mixed with Crimson Alizarin it will give the lovely grey-green of some willow trees or the colour of the bark of beech trees. Use Olive Green on its own and not mixed with other colours as it is already a mixture of Raw Sienna and Winsor Blue and is handy as a short cut. It is not advisable to mix Payne's Grey too often as it is already a mixture, but with a yellow mixed it will give a subtle green. It is a gentle colour and useful for monochromes. It can be included in a three colour palette, the other two being Light Red and Raw Sienna which gives a subdued unity to the landscape. Brown Madder has been included in the colour mixing charts in Figure 27, so that Burnt Sienna will not be repeated in the second and third grid. This is a good colour for use in landscapes as it is not so pink as Crimson Alizarin, and will make interesting mixtures as you will find when you complete the colour charts.

Terre Verte, a gentle, bluish green can be added to the palette later but needs mixing well and kept stirred as it is slightly sticky. Scarlet Lake is lovely to have as an extra colour, being a bright, transparent, warm red. Other colours will be needed for flower painting and these will be mentioned in that context.

Although beginning with only a few colours it is advisable to buy artists' quality rather than students'. This is even more important in watercolour than in oil. Although the Artists' Colourmen do an excellent job with the students' quality paints and they are more than adequate at the beginning, gradually replace them with the artists' quality and you will see a difference. Earth colours such as Yellow Ochre, Raw and Burnt Umber, Raw and Burnt Sienna, Light, Venetian and Indian Red are very much the same in either quality.

At the time of writing, I hear that Cobalt Blue is difficult to obtain, due to the mines being flooded. This means that it will be an expensive colour to purchase. If it is likely to be a permanent shortage, a good substitute for it would be Manganese Blue, a clear, light blue, but bright. This probably applies to Coerulum Blue also as it is a Cobalt stannate.

Is there a place for white in watercolour?

I think white can be used judiciously where wanted, such as in the fine work necessary for birds' plumage or to enhance a mast catching the light. Some artists take out small lights with a sharp knife but this can only be done on good hand-made paper. Using white depends upon whether you are a 'purist' or not, but it might be as well for a beginner to avoid it and concentrate on transparent watercolour until really experienced, otherwise it will be like wearing water wings too long when learning to swim. The moment of jumping in at the deep end and striking out will be put off.

Paper

The kinds of paper to be used in this medium are very important. Different effects will be obtained depending on how the watercolour is used on different papers. Good art shops will supply most papers but, when one becomes sufficiently experienced, it is more economical to buy in bulk from the paper mills. It can be kept for one's own use or to divide among painting friends. The best papers are hand-made from rag and the cheaper kinds are made from wood pulp. The hand-made papers will have a deckle edge and a water mark and are, of course, more expensive than the machine-made paper. The wood pulp papers were inclined to turn yellow with age but with modern technology, this is no longer the case and they can be used with confidence. The rag papers are usually hard, sized and resilient and most useful for direct painting, that is, painting which is put down in correct tonal and colour values in the first instance and left, rather than being built up in washes. Wood pulp papers are softer and lend themselves to atmospheric washes more than the harder varieties. The mould-made papers are largely made by Inveresk now and of these, Bockingford and Saunders are those most often used.

Hand-made paper

J. Barcham Green are the major manufacturers of hand-made paper in England and their papers include Green's Pasteless Board, Crisbrook, RWS and J. Green. Hand-made papers are usually produced with three different surfaces and in different weights. It is useful to have this information because students tell me that assistants in art shops sometimes do not know what they are selling and cannot give advice. The surfaces are called NOT, HOT-PRESSED, and ROUGH. A 'rough' surface is more difficult for a beginner to use. It needs a bold approach with a large brush, as much of the surface of the paper is left where the brush has skated over it. A 'not' surface is one that has not been hot-pressed and is the one most suitable and the most often used for watercolour painting. 'Hot-pressed' is the smoothest paper and is best for line-and-wash and pen-and-ink work.

'Arches' is a hand-made French paper which is delightful to use but is not always easy to get, only being sold in some art shops. Fabriano, also is a good hand-made Italian paper. Buy it when the opportunity occurs.

Weight of paper and stretching

As to weight, at the time of writing, it is still referred to as lbs per ream for Imperial size and for this definition the weights are 72 lbs, 90 lbs, 140 lbs, 200 lbs, and 300 lbs. Any paper below and including 140 lbs will need stretching before beginning to paint, of which, more later. Paper sizes are changing gradually however, and the relevant weights to the new A sizes will be 154 g/m², 192 g/m², 300 g/m², 428 g/m², 642 g/m².

Bockingford and some kinds of Saunders papers do not need stretching, whatever their weight. In fact it would do more harm than good as their surfaces are very tender, so it is largely the hand-made papers that need stretching, in order to stop them cockling. Bockingford 200 lb is a very pleasant paper to work on and is used by some of the best modern watercolourists, though others dislike it. A lot depends upon the method of painting, whether it becomes a favourite of yours or not. Good cartridge paper can be used by those experienced in the medium, with successful results, but the paper may yellow with age, so is not recommended for permanence.

Surface of paper

The influence of watercolour on different surfaces is shown in Figure 5.

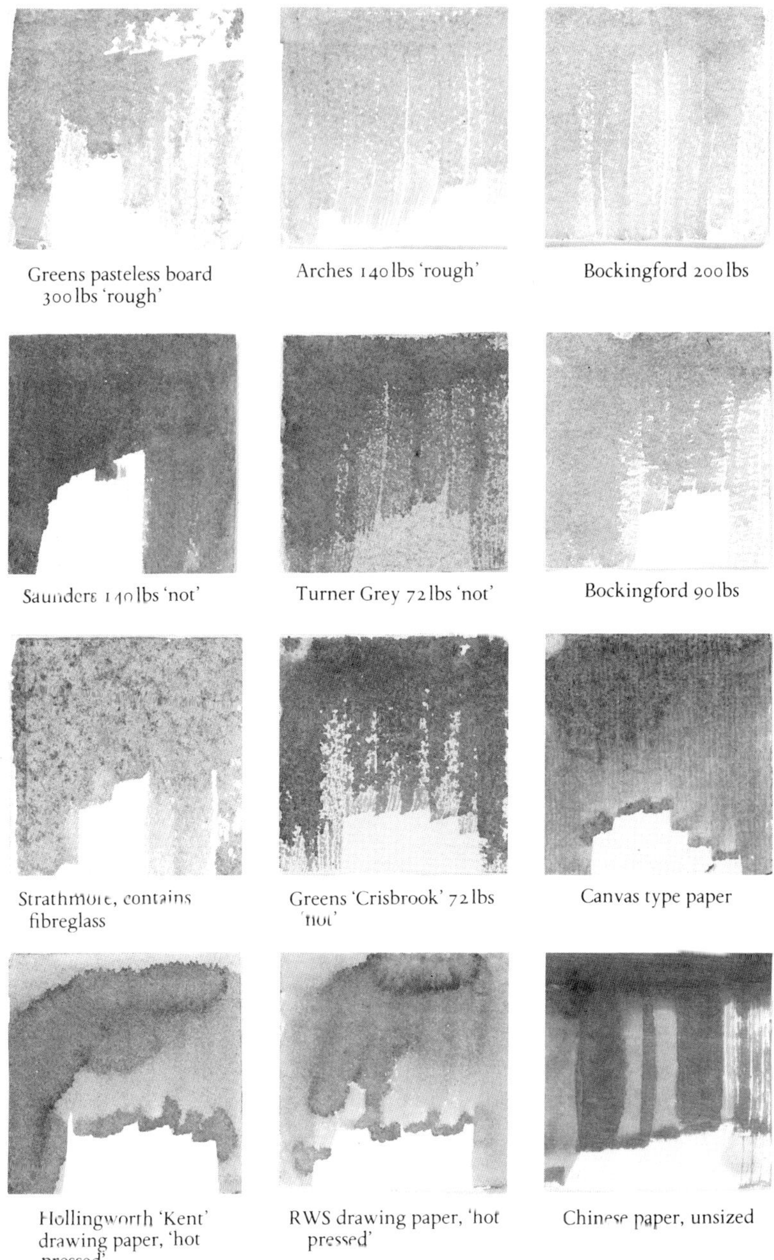

Figure 5 The effect of watercolour on different papers

New papers are coming on to the market all the time and it is a good idea to buy only a small quantity until you have found out if it suits you. Paper is cheaper to buy by the sheet than as a pad, though of course pads and sketch books are more convenient to carry about. Although Green's Pasteless Boards are very expensive, they can be used on both sides, do not need stretching and are lovely to work on. Sometimes hand-made papers seem to resist the watercolour and this is due to the size on the surface. All it needs is a gentle sponge over with clean water before beginning to paint. The correct side upon which to work of any paper is the roughest. If hand-made papers are held up to the light the name will be seen as a watermark and the right side for reading that will be the correct side of the paper. The mould-made papers will not have a watermark but if held horizontal to the light the roughest surface can easily be seen. Oil painting paper can be used by those wishing to experiment, as the priming on the paper will repel the watercolour and some interesting effects can be obtained. If you should come across a 'cache' of Whatman paper overlooked somewhere buy it up at once, as this excellent paper has not been made for some years. It is lovely paper and some elderly relatives may still have some 'up their sleeves'.

Tinted paper

Although the white of the paper is the basis of watercolours sometimes it is interesting to use a slightly tinted one. David Cox and De Wint are pale buff papers and Turner Grey is a blue-grey. These papers do not need stretching and will give a subdued, harmonious picture, suitable for some subjects, but some of the brilliance is lost through not being on white. The tinted papers are very attractive, however, if used with gouache and can play an important part in the painting.

Brushes

Many beginners find watercolour more difficult than it need be because the brush is too small. A good wash simply cannot be put on with a small brush. Ideally, a Kolinsky sable, Number 12, is the best all round brush to buy, but the prices at the moment are astronomical and good substitutes can be found. The Daler Dylon brushes, made of nylon, are very good indeed as are the Tip Point nylon brushes, by Winsor and Newton, in large, medium and small sizes. One disadvantage of nylon brushes is that they do not hold as much water as sables nor do they lift off paint as well. Another good substitute for sable is ox hair, or ox-ear hair. These do not come to such a good point but serve very well and do not wear out quite so quickly. Never buy camel, squirrel, or just 'hair'. These brushes will have no resilience and will not spring back to shape when lifted from the paper. Although one good sable will do nearly everything, it is preferable to have several brushes from which to choose for specific effects. Round brushes are more popular because they hold more paint than flat ones, but flat ones are considerably

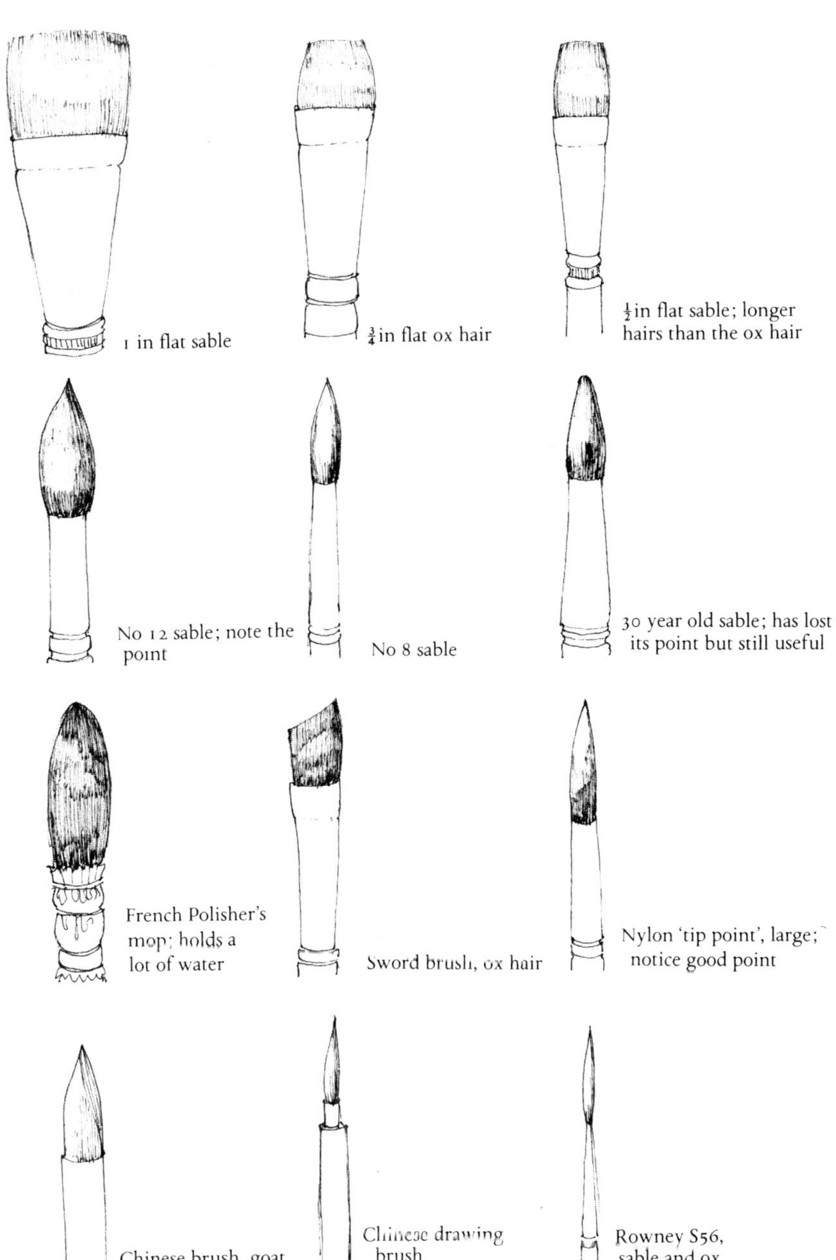

Figure 6 Shapes of different brushes

15

cheaper. A French Polisher's mop is a useful brush to have if you can find one. They are not very easy to track down, but are worth hunting for because they will hold so much paint.

Of the round brushes, the sizes which are most useful are No 12, No 8 and No 2. A number S56 Sable and Ox, made by Rowneys, is excellent for small detail and 'twiggery'.

Of the flat brushes, a 1 in sable is a joy to use and a $\frac{1}{2}$ in is a useful extra. A sword brush is handy for buildings, corners and so on and can be seen in Figure 6, which shows a selection of brushes. The round sables should come to a true and delicate point when immersed in water, and in the old days, one was allowed to test this out in the shop. The 30-year-old sable which is shown in Figure 6 is still an old friend. Although it has lost its point, a great deal of watercolour painting is done on the side of the brush and it is still very useful for this.

A small eye sponge, bought at any good chemist, is also useful, not only for washing over the paper or washing in skies, but for lifting areas of paint that are too wet, and for cleaning the palette.

Keeping brushes

Brushes need to be looked after and the points protected at all times. Brush cases can be bought, but one of the best is home-made. Buy a raffia dinner mat, the kind that will roll up easily, from a chain store, sew a piece of elastic across by stitching down at intervals of a brush width. Place the brushes in the slots provided, roll up and fasten with an elastic band and the brush tips will be satisfactorily protected.

Don't keep brushes hidden away in drawers or the moth will get at them. When not in use, keep them upright in a jar and examine them frequently for signs of moth and dust.

Further equipment

Many people take to watercolour because the equipment is less burdensome than that required for oil, but find once they have made the change that they enjoy it more and find it a challenge. Of course, it has its frustrations, but the most important attribute for this medium is patience, because washes must be allowed to dry to the required state before proceeding with the next stage of the picture.

Indoors

The paints, brushes, sponge and paper have been described. The only other pieces of equipment necessary are a board, which can be of hardboard for lightness, about 1 in larger than the usual size of your paper, a water pot, bull-dog clips and a large piece of cotton rag. Tissues will not do because they become too saturated. Add a soft pencil and a sharpener and this is all the equipment needed for someone who is housebound or who does not wish to venture outside in the cold winter weather. The board can be propped on a box on a table so an easel will not be necessary.

Outdoors

For out-of-doors painting a little more will be needed. A small stool will be necessary if you wish to sit. Sometimes one can sit on the ground but it may be impossible to see your subject from there. If you can stand, so much the better. You will need a sketching easel if you are standing, but on a low stool, equipment can be placed on the ground within easy reach. If a support for the board is wanted, either a knee easel, or a stick easel, can be used, both of which are inexpensive. It is an advantage not to have the board clamped down too firmly as you may wish to swivel the painting round in order for the wash to flow in another direction. When out-of-doors a large polythene bottle full of water will need to be taken in order to replace the dirty water frequently. A tote bag will hold all the gear, plus a lightweight waterproof and rain hat, vacuum flask and sandwiches. The easel can be carried under one arm unless it is either the stick or knee easel. Either of these fold up quite small and will go in the bag. Instead of the tote bag, a special-purpose sketching bag can be purchased to which the larger type sketching easel can be strapped, and the whole thing can be carried over one shoulder. If standing and using a larger sketching easel, a hollow rubber ball with a piece cut out and threaded with string is useful, hung on the front of the easel, to contain the water and save you from continually bending down.

The importance of drawing

Being able to draw correctly is more important in watercolour than in any other medium because there is a limit to the corrections that can be made, either in a preliminary pencil drawing, or in what is called 'brush drawing'. In order to keep the freshness, a statement must be made and kept to, with the minimum of alteration. This means that nothing must be put down until it has been thought about. Students often tell me that they can't draw, but find that they can when they approach it from the right angle.

Using a viewfinder

An aid to drawing is a small view-finder. It need only be a small rectangle, about 40×25 mm ($1\frac{1}{2} \times 1$ in), in a large sheet of paper about a small sketch book size so that you can't see round the edge and be distracted from the small area in the view-finder. A small hole is better than a large because too much can be seen too easily through the larger one. Several of these view-finders can be cut to different measurements, relative to the size of the paper being used, as, obviously, a square hole will contain a different composition from that required for a long oblong of paper. The closer the aperture is held to the eye, the bigger the area which will be seen beyond. Held at a distance from the eye, a cluster of wild flowers in the foreground could be the subject of the picture. Whatever the decision, try to hold the view-finder at the same distance from the eye until it is no longer necessary.

To begin, hold the view-finder at the required distance from your eye, to enclose the picture which you wish to portray. Choose an object somewhere near the centre of the composition and decide how large it is in relation to the rest of the picture and its precise place within it. This is the most difficult decision and after this, things become easier. Having decided on size and place, draw it on the paper, relative to how it appears in the view-finder. From now on, referring back to the view-finder, work outwards from the object already drawn, and assess each line, angle and size as you go along. Take thought before putting anything down and you will find that the whole comes together rather like a jig-saw, but the most important thing to remember is to work from the inside out. I hope this will not only help you to draw more easily but that you may come to enjoy it.

Drawing with ball-pen

Another thing that is a help to anyone learning to draw is a ball-pen. Not a fibre-tip pen or a felt pen but a fine, indelible ball-pen. Later, when drawing comes easily, pencils of different grades can be used, but for anyone beginning to draw, it is essential that it should be with something that cannot be erased and will give a fine line with precision. If you cannot rub out your mistakes, more thought will be taken before putting down a line. If a mistake is made, leave the line and put in the correct one. When the drawing is finished, any mistakes, providing there are not too many, will be incorporated into the whole and will be unnoticed.

Making a start with painting

At any important exhibition of watercolours, many styles will be seen, but all of them will have a transparency and clean colour. This does not rule out rich colour, as can be seen from the examples of artists' work shown at the beginning of the book. A gouache will have more solidity and be more akin to oils, because the colour is opaque, but even here there will be a fluid approach rather than one of building up, as in oil painting. It is a mistake to take a watercolour too far. So often, a student, or a professional for that matter, will do a lovely painting, leaving something to the imagination of the beholder, but will then proceed to spoil it by crossing the *t*'s and dotting the *i*'s. Some artists can take a watercolour to a final conclusion successfully in great detail, but something of the medium is lost in this virtuosity.

Different techniques

Watercolour can be approached with a free style, laying on the washes with no previous pencil drawing as shown in Figure 7. In a more detailed picture, incorporating buildings or boats, some preliminary pencil work may be necessary and the drawing will need to be approached with more care. A subject of this kind is shown in Figure 8.

Sometimes dry brushwork is used, but usually combined with other methods; it is rarely used on its own. An example of this is shown in Figure 9, where it has been used over dry paint. Another method which is not used so much in modern paintings, but which is interesting to experiment with, is superimposing one colour over another, waiting for each wash to dry, in between. In effect, glazes are built up and brilliant colour is achieved, which can be useful when portraying flowers.

Figure 10 shows the effect of lifting out paint from a wet wash with a sponge and Figure 11 shows the effect of dropping wet paint into a slightly damp wash.

Figure 12 shows a 'brush drawing', a description which is self explanatory. It is useful to use black Indian ink, both neat and diluted for practising this technique as you have to work very directly without second thoughts, but plenty of 'first thoughts'.

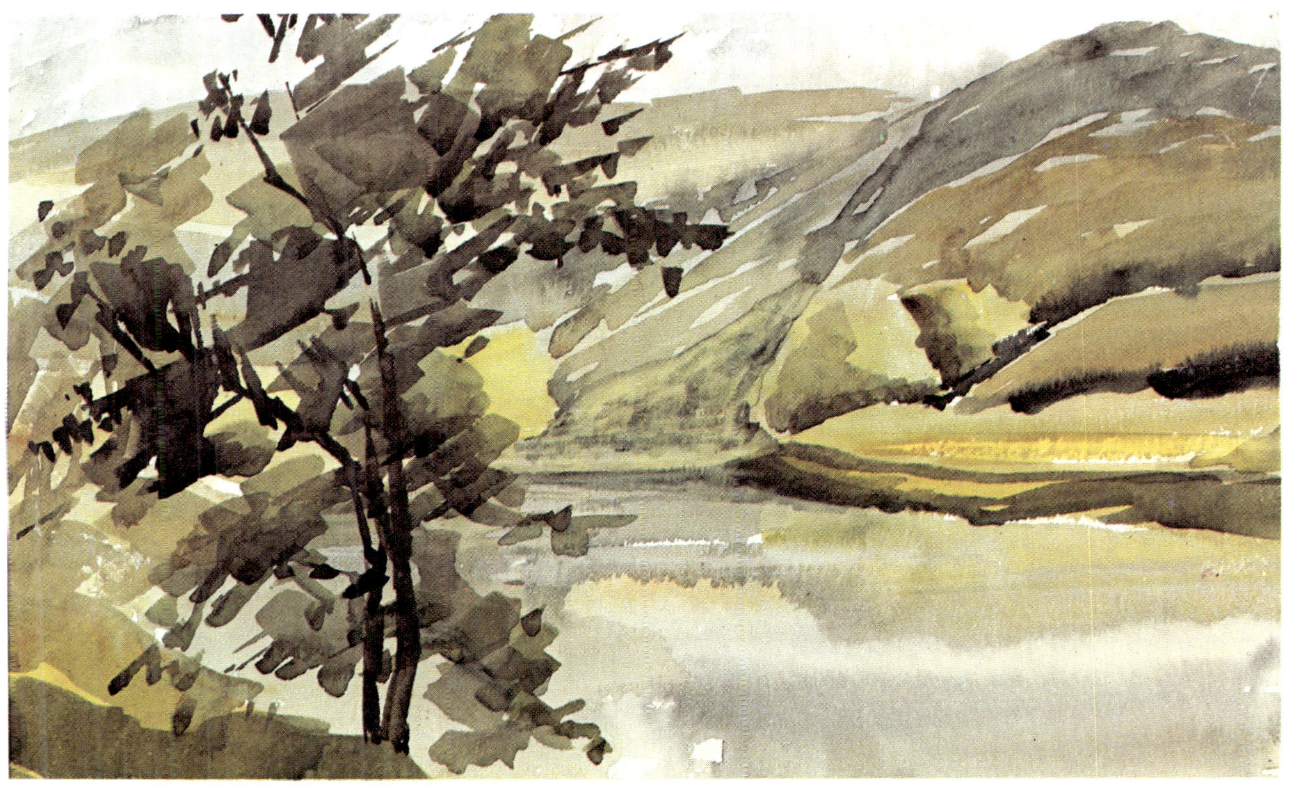

Figure 7 Free and broad style of painting with minimal detail

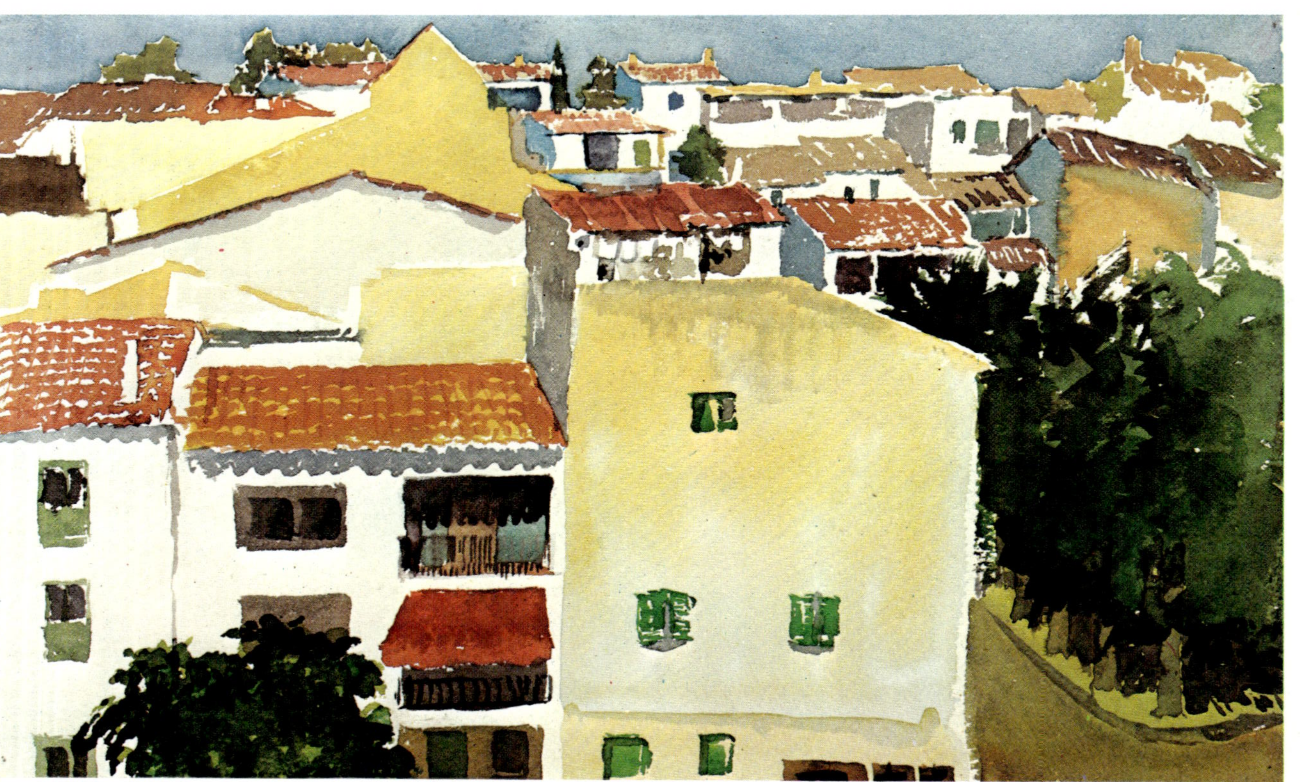

Figure 8 More detailed structure so a little preliminary pencil work could be useful

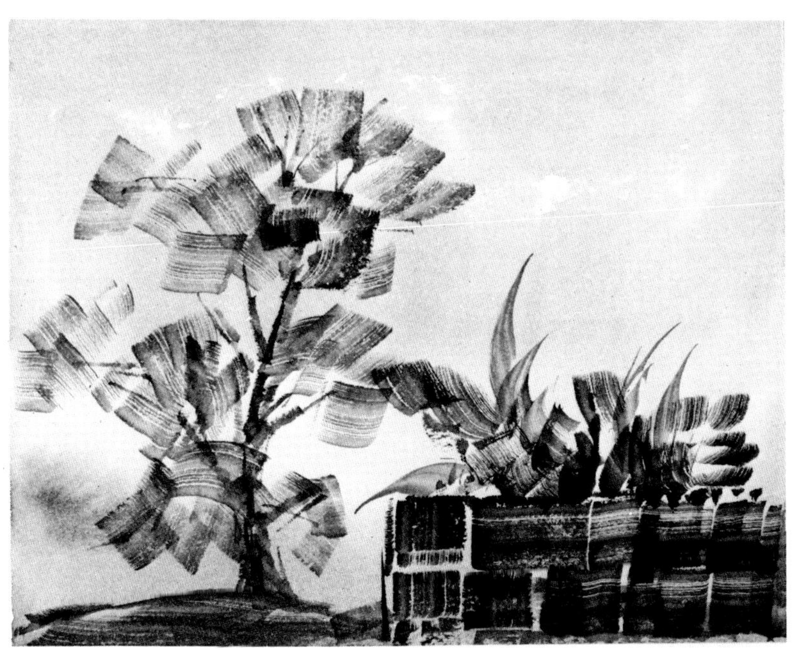

Figure 9   Dry brush (flat) used over dry paint

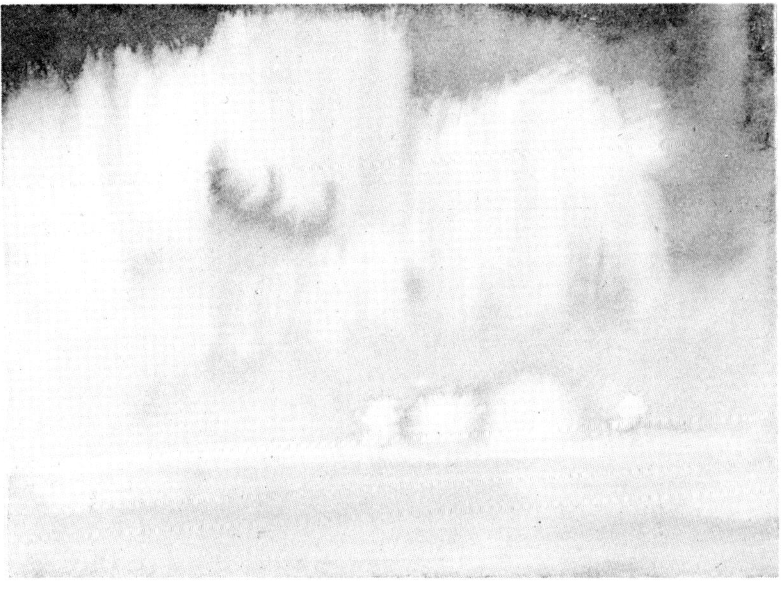

Figure 10   Lifting out with a sponge while still damp

23

Figure 11   'Dropping in' while previous wash is still damp

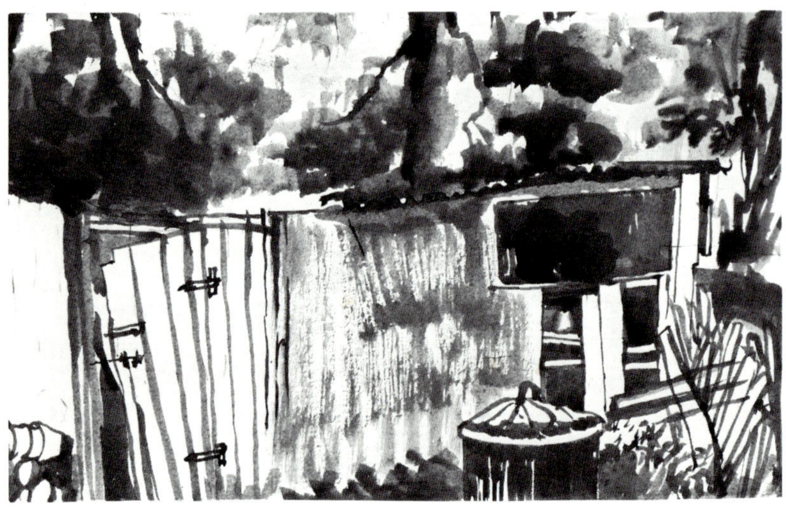

Figure 12   Drawing directly with the brush, ie brush drawing

Laying a flat wash

It is useful to practise these different effects for yourself but before doing so it will be necessary to learn to lay a flat wash. It may not be used all that often in picture-making but it is the basis of a good watercolour technique, and is not so easy as it may at first appear. In Figure 13 will be seen a flat wash carried out in Light Red and in Figure 14 one done in French Ultramarine. Notice how the French Ultramarine has granulated which is caused by the pigment particles separating in the water. This happens with some colours more than others and can be made use of for certain effects, but it can be tiresome if it is not wanted, in which case another but equivalent colour can be used. When you have learnt to lay a flat wash and a gradated one, it is good exercise to practise laying washes with all the colours in your palette in order to find out which colours run quickly and which are inclined to granulate, which is useful information as well as getting to know what each colour looks like on its own.

To practise a flat wash take a piece of 'not' paper or, more simply, a piece of Bockingford of the same weight, size about 20 × 15 cm (8 × 6 in). Lay it on the board and fasten, either with drawing pins or a bull-dog clip. Tilt the board slightly, so that the wash can run down the paper but not too quickly. Make up a solution of pigment and water in a painting well or a saucer, making sure that there is more mixture than seems necessary to cover the paper. If there is not sufficient, the wash will dry while mixing more and will be spoilt by having a hard line through the middle of it apart from the difficulty of matching the colour. Often, a student's first attempts are too pale. This is because allowance has not been made for the fact that watercolour can dry fifty per cent lighter than when put on the paper. Until experience is gained, always put the colour on much darker than would be thought necessary. Knowledge will come with practice. Remember at all times to keep the board slightly tilted.

Having made up the colour and stirred it well, take the largest brush and fill it with the mixture. Take the brush lightly across the top of the paper without lifting it. When the end is reached lift the brush, dip it into the mixture, and, beginning again on the left, overlap the first stroke of paint by $\frac{1}{2}$ cm and carry it to the end of the paper as before. Continue this exercise until you reach the bottom of the paper, squeeze the brush dry and lift any surplus paint with it, from the bottom of the wash, otherwise it will bleed back and spoil it. The way of laying the wash is shown in Figure 15 but you will notice that the wash has bled back because it was not taken to the bottom and mopped up.

Gradated wash

The next thing to tackle is a gradated wash as shown in Figures 16 and 17. You will notice that in Figure 16 the wash is not as even as it might be, and this is because it is more difficult to achieve with some pigments. In Figure

Figure 13 Flat wash using Light Red

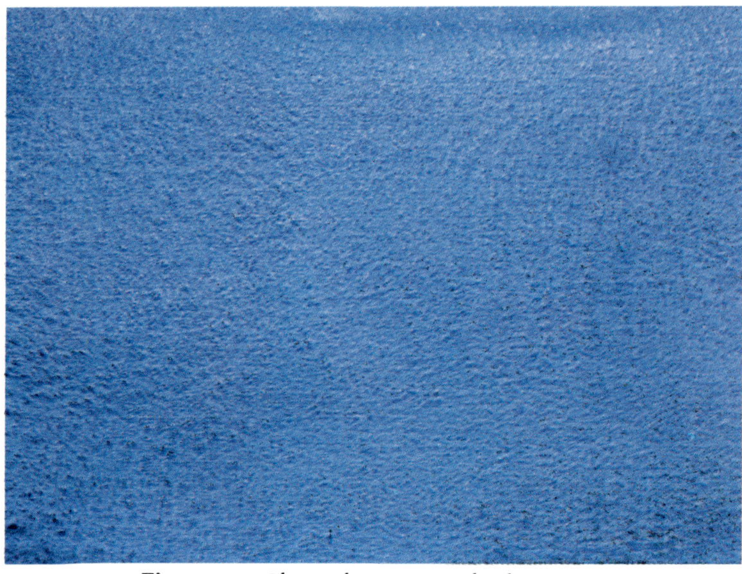

Figure 14 Flat wash using French Ultramarine

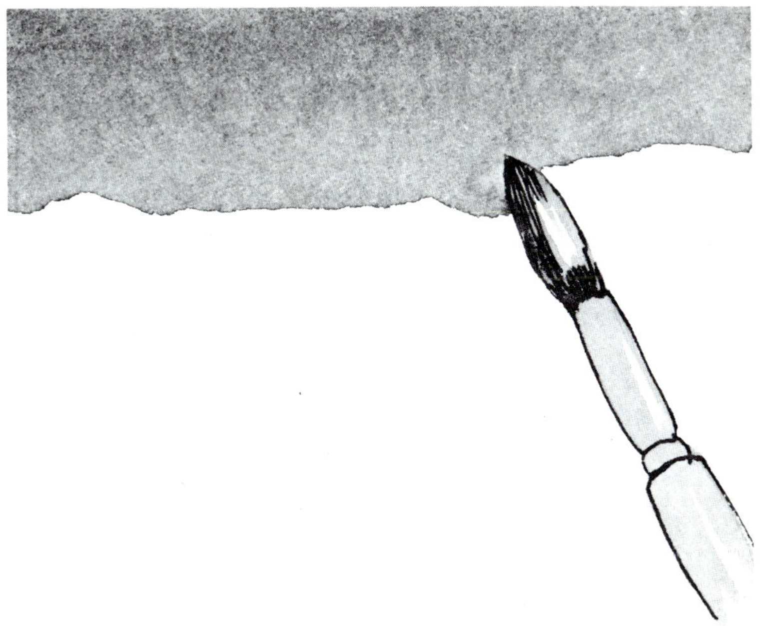

Figure 15   How to apply a flat wash

17, one drop of detergent or washing up liquid has been added to the water which has made it easier to get an evenly gradated wash.

A gradated wash will be used quite often when a morning or evening or a cloudless sky is wanted. It will be noticed, when you begin to look at skies for painting, that, unless there is low-lying cloud or mist, the sky will appear lighter and warmer at the horizon than it is at the zenith. For the gradated wash, mix the colour as before and brush it lightly across the top of the paper. Before beginning the next line of wash, dip the brush into a little water and take it across the previous line of paint as before. Before beginning each line, dip the brush lightly into the water so that the wash gets weaker as it comes down the paper.

Variegated wash

Now try a variegated wash as shown in Figure 18. The colours used in this were Prussian Blue, Winsor Green, Light Red and New Gamboge. It can be very pleasing to have a variegated wash over the whole picture, into which to paint, and this will give a diffuse, atmospheric start which can be developed afterwards with stronger tones and details. In order to lay the wash, have three different colours mixed up in separate saucers and change the colours as the wash is taken down the page. It helps to keep the colours unsullied if three different brushes are used.

Figure 16 Some pigments make an even gradated wash hard to achieve

Figure 17 One drop of detergent in the water will help

Figure 18   Showing a variegated wash

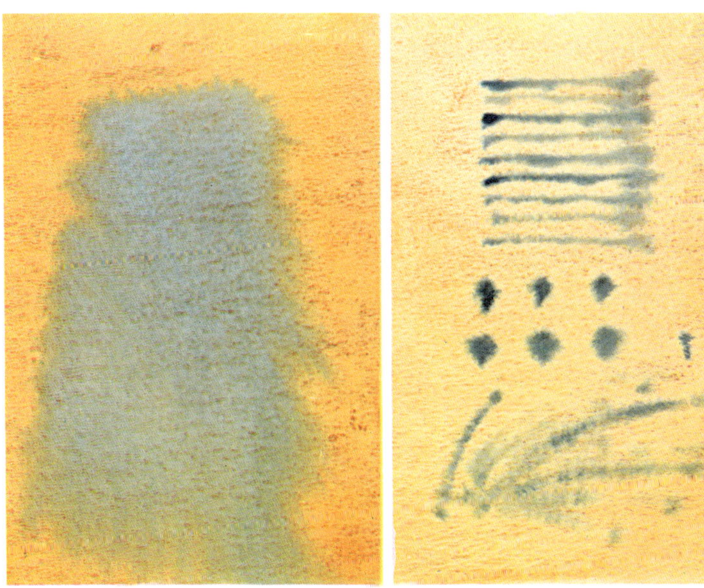

Figure 19   Paint, too wet, dropped into wet paint

Figure 20   Dry paint dropped into wet paint

Figure 21   Superimposing Cobalt Blue over Light Red

Figure 22   Mixing Cobalt Blue and Light Red

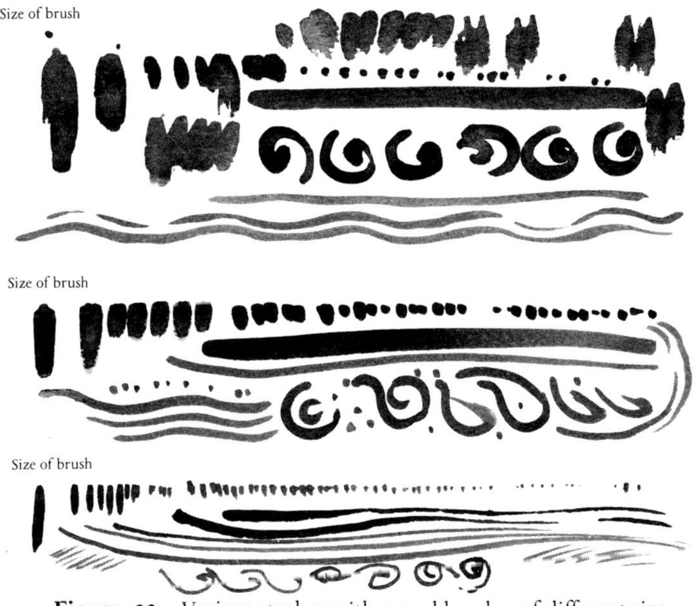

Size of brush

Size of brush

Size of brush

Figure 23   Various strokes with round brushes of different size

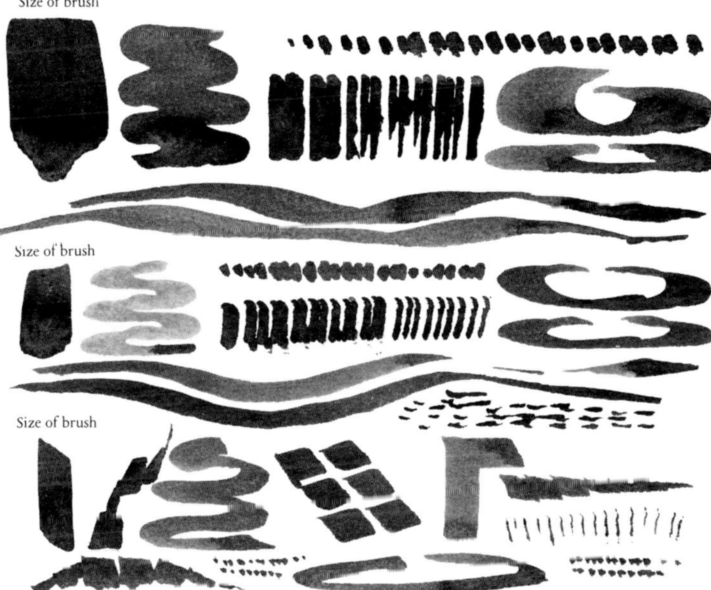

Size of brush

Size of brush

Size of brush

Figure 24   Various strokes with flat brushes of different size

Figure 25 Round brush pulled quickly across rough paper with more or less water

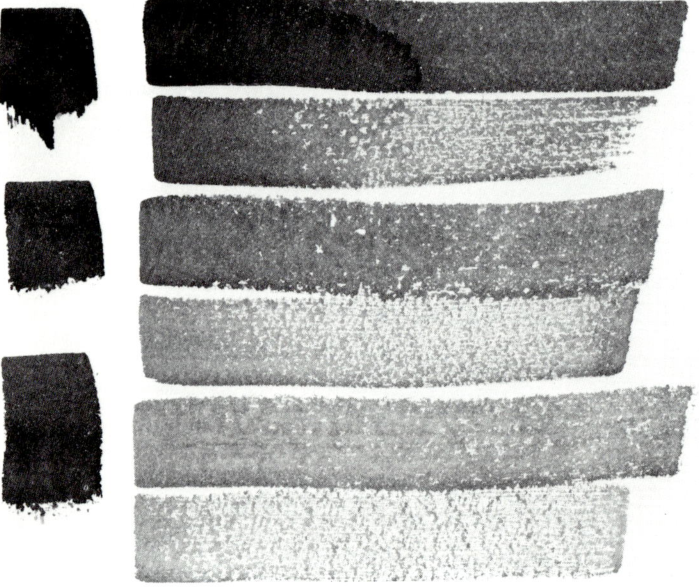

Figure 26 Flat brush pulled quickly across rough paper with more or less water

Dropping in

Another useful exercise is to lay a flat wash and drop another colour into it at different stages of drying. This experiment will help later in showing how to control a wash. In Figure 19 Prussian Blue is dropped into Raw Sienna while the first wash of Raw Sienna was still very wet. The Prussian Blue has also been diluted with water so there is a feathering out and loss of contour and colour, but if the Prussian Blue is dropped in almost dry, it will not spread too far and can be controlled. This is shown in Figure 20.

Superimposing

The next exercise is in superimposing. Some painters say that all water-colour painting should be direct, that is, mixing the washes to the right tone and colour, putting them down and leaving them alone. This is an excellent method, making for cleanliness and transparency but, used exclusively, it cuts off a whole lot of different experiences to be tried in this sympathetic and sensitive medium. I have found that with superimposing, one can often get a more luminous effect than with direct mixtures and in Figure 21 this is shown by laying in a gradated wash of Light Red. When quite dry, a wash of Cobalt Blue has been superimposed. In Figure 22 the wash is put on with the same two colours mixed together, giving quite a different result, but just as viable.

Brush exercises

Having acquired some skill in applying paint in washes, now is the time to try out some exercises using different brushes.

In Figure 23 you can see various strokes and effects obtained with round brushes, including the French Polisher's mop and in Figure 24 you can see the results of using a 1 in sable brush. Some are obtained by using more water and others with a drier brush. If you try them yourself you will find out which is which. Figure 25 shows the effect of a brush containing only slightly moist pigment, drawn rapidly over a rough paper and Figure 26 shows the same thing done with a flat brush.

Painting a monochrome

The first exercise in actual picture-making is going to be in monochrome. Not because it is easier than using colour but because it gives an early lesson in tonal values, aerial perspective and the actual use of watercolour. Aerial perspective is due to layers of atmosphere between us and the different planes of the scene contemplated, which in effect, act as gauzy curtains. The far distance will be paler than the middle distance, and the foreground will be stronger in tone than either. The same principle applies when using colour, being paler and greyer in the far distance and becoming brighter, stronger and warmer in the foreground. A shadow in the foreground will be darker than one farther back and a shaft of sunlight across the foreground will be *brighter* than the sunshine in the middle distance but not lighter. If you remember 'brighter not lighter', it is a help, as it takes some time for the penny to drop.

This is not easy to show in monochrome so in Figure 27 the foreground

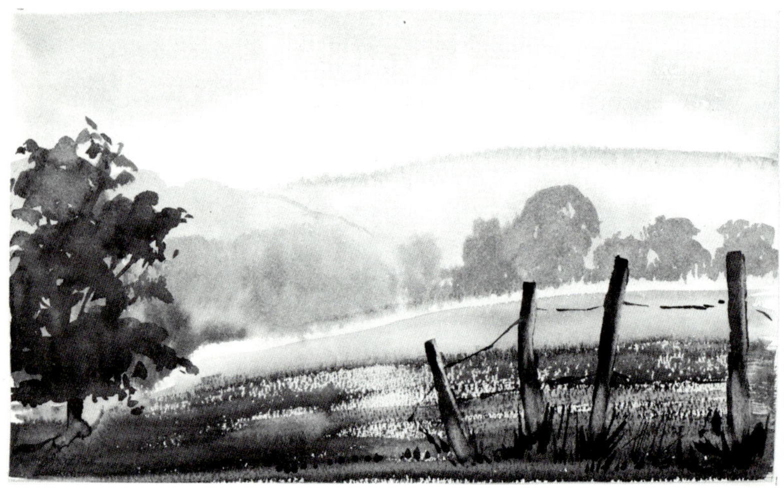

Figure 27 Completed monochrome

is shown as darker in tone than the middle distance. Sometimes, due to cloud formation and other atmospheric effects, a band of trees will appear very dark in the distance, but the thing to do is to compare it with the darks in the foreground, which will not only be darker but warmer in colour as well.

To try the monochrome, take a piece of paper, size about 29 × 38 cm (11 × 15 in) which is the old quarter-Imperial size (the new A sizes are slightly different). Using a large brush or the eye sponge, wet the paper gently from the top to the bottom with clean water. Dampening the paper before painting depends on the subject that is being painted and the atmosphere. In a hot, dry room or in hot sun, the preliminary dampening will help the washes not to dry too quickly, but on a damp day the washes will take so long to dry anyway that it will be more of a hindrance. A misty, undefined subject, such as that in Figure 27, will gain from being worked on damp paper but a more precise and detailed subject will need to be painted on dry paper. Having laid the wash of clean water, hold the paper at eye-level as you will be able to see, at this angle, the shine on the paper. When this has disappeared, lay the paper down and you are ready to start. Have ready a large pan, full of diluted Payne's Grey and, by the side, a spare piece of watercolour paper on which to try out the colour before using it. In watercolour we work from light to dark, which is the opposite from oil painting, and remember that it is going to dry very much lighter. There are a few brave souls who paint their darks in first, but I don't advise this for beginners, otherwise you will be in the soup in more ways than one.

When the paper is at the right stage, with the largest brush, lay in the lightest wash, which is the sky, taking it right down behind the trees,

Figure 28 How to work out a sequence of washes on a quick sketch

gradually reverting to water with no pigment, to the bottom of the page. Now wait until the shine has disappeared from the paper again and drop in the far distance, making the colour a little stronger, ie using less water to pigment, and the paper will probably be about right for dropping in the middle distance trees, but if not, wait until it is a little drier. Successful watercolour technique relies largely on patience as I have already said, but it cannot be said too often. Next, the stronger-toned tree on the left, in the nearer plane will go in, and then the foreground. Last to go in are the posts which are dark, being in the immediate foreground but note that they are lighter at the base, because some light will be reflected upwards from the ground; this applies also to the tree trunk. Although this is a simple picture, with no details, it will aid good habits and help in more difficult pictures. Get into the habit, before beginning to paint, of giving some thought to the sequence of washes remembering that you will be working from light to dark. In Figure 28 a sketch shows the tones pencilled in as a reminder before beginning the finished painting. At this point it is useful to note the importance of only pencilling in these tones. It is not always easy to predict accurate results and mistakes are often made when numbering. Another thing to remember is to use the side of the brush for painting masses, particularly skies and foliage and foregrounds, as it will keep the painting broad and prevent 'tightness'.

Beginning with colour

Colour mixing

Before using colour, something must be learnt about mixing it. Although making your own colour charts may appear, at first sight, time-consuming and tedious, it is not so. Figure 29 shows three grids. For the sake of simplicity, take only five colours along each side, but the grids can be extended when colours are added to the palette. Each colour is laid down in the relevant square, by itself, without being mixed with anything else and this is a good way of getting to know the hue of all your colours. Then each colour in the horizontal row is mixed in turn with each colour from the vertical row, adding water to each to show a lighter tone. The charts should be self-explanatory but the first one will give greens, the next will show greys, purples and some dark green, and the third will give reds, oranges and browns. These mixtures will take you along the road to colour mixing but there is always more exploration to be made by anyone willing to learn. Do not add any extras however until these have been fully explored, and when they are added, find out what they will do with the other colours so that gradually more knowledge is acquired, and confusion is avoided. As you will see, only the first row in the charts has been mixed, so that curiosity will drive you on to complete them yourself and by so doing, among other things, you will find out which mixtures produce dirty painting as well as those which give clean, transparent tints. One thing to realize is that as more or less of one colour is mixed to another so the resulting colour will vary, which is why a watercolour can never be copied exactly as to colour. No formula can be given but knowledge comes with practice.

Painting sky

Before painting a landscape, it will be easier and more relaxing to paint a sky, with a minimal piece of landscape dropped in at the end. Figure 30 shows a cloudless sky, usually seen in the early morning in Britain, both in summer and winter. It is laid in with a gradated wash of Raw Sienna. When

This chart will show pinks, oranges and browns but some greys

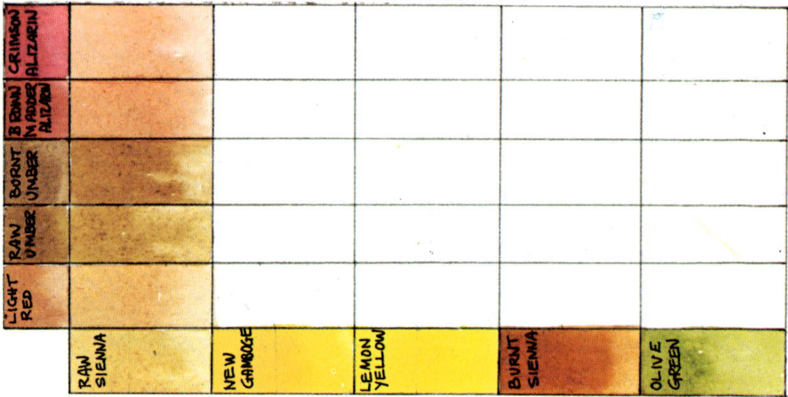

This chart will show mainly greys but some purples. The mixture of Winsor Green and
Crimson Alizarin has been shown in colour to show how attractive it is

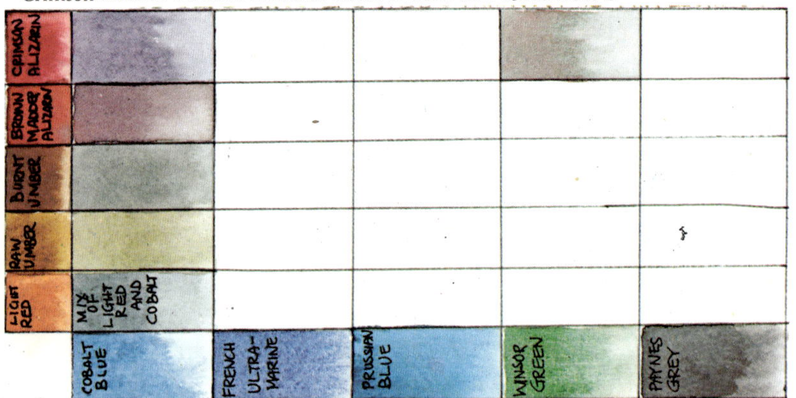

This chart will show mainly greens but some greys

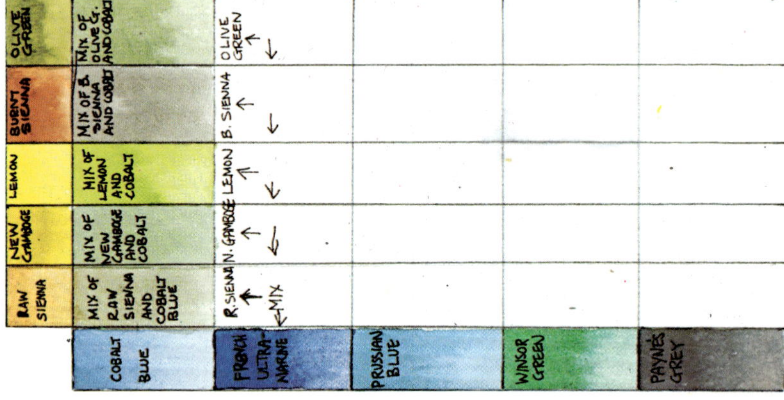

Figure 29 Colour charts

38

this is dry, the paper is turned upside down and a gradated wash of Scarlet Lake is laid on top, the Raw Sienna shining through the Scarlet Lake. Turning the paper the right way up and while still damp, run in a few silhouetted trees in Burnt Umber, standing out dark against the luminous sky.

For a second sky choose one, often seen in Britain in all seasons, which is basically blue with cumulus clouds. Figure 31 shows a diagram of the perspective of the clouds with regard to size and distance from each other. Also note that cumulus clouds in the middle and far distance are straight at the bottom edge. These are the kind of things that will be learnt gradually from observing and drawing constantly. No rules are rigid in nature's spectacles and one is continually being surprised with unexpected effects. The colour perspective will give more brilliant and warmer colour at the zenith, immediately above us, and paler, cooler colour at the horizon, generally speaking, but this is often contradicted by the sky at the horizon appearing warmer, due to atmospheric conditions, so the moral of this is, that one must look and see and remember.

For Figure 32 mix up some Cobalt and a little Light Red. Pencil in the cloud shapes lightly and dampen the paper. Wait for the shine to disappear and drop in a strong solution of colour, keeping the white areas of pencilled clouds free of paint. As the paper is damp, the edges of the clouds will be

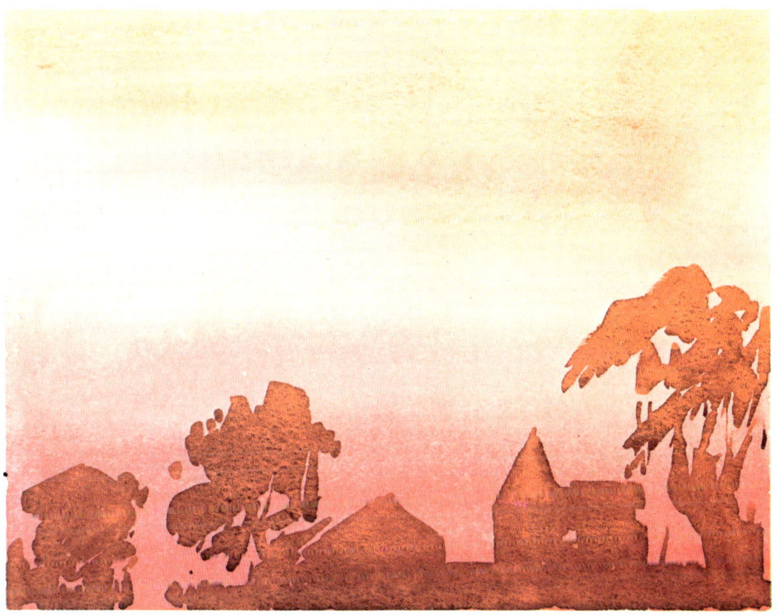

Figure 30 Morning sky; Scarlet Lake superimposed over Raw Sienna

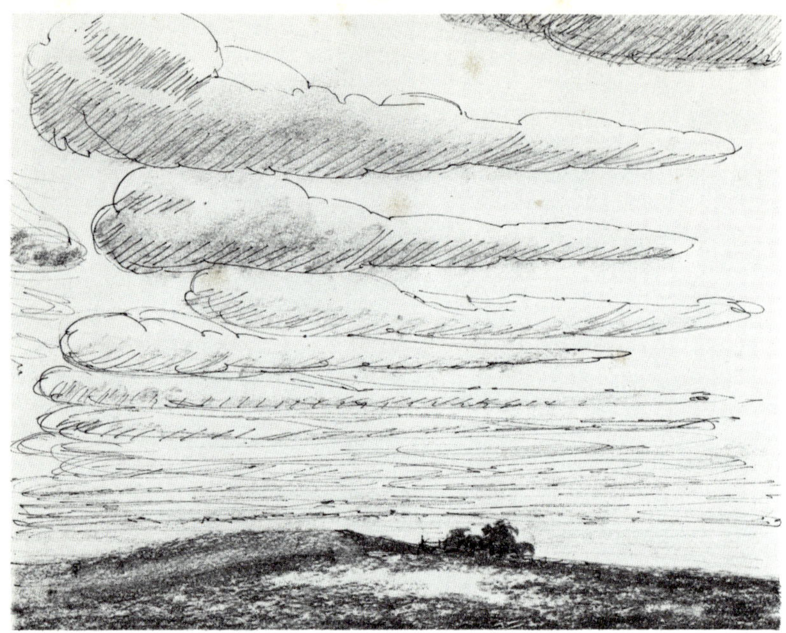

Figure 31   Perspective of clouds

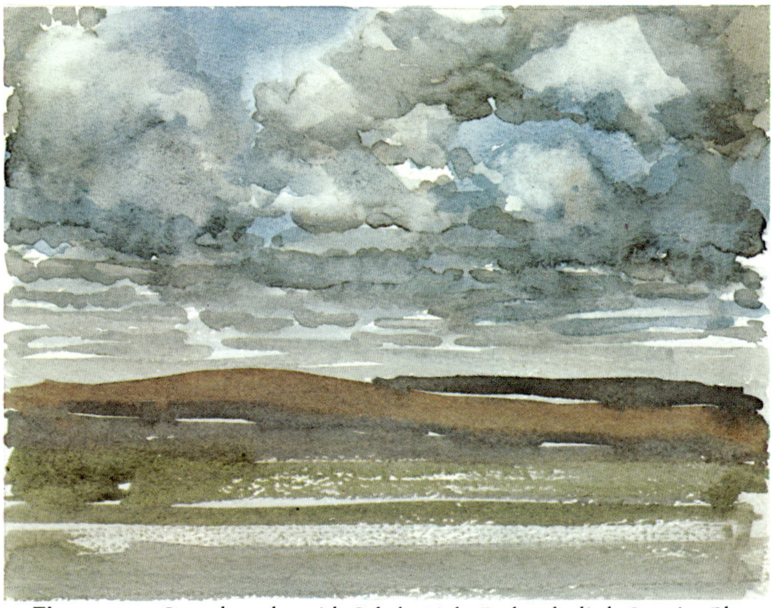

Figure 32   Cumulous sky with Cobalt, Light Red and a little Prussian Blue

soft but able to be controlled. As the wash comes down the paper, add a little Prussian Blue to the mixture and also some water to lighten the colour. Further down still, add a touch of Light Red and again, a little water. While the paper is still damp, drop in the shadow colour of the clouds which is a stronger mixture of Cobalt and Light Red than that used for the grey-blue sky. A touch of very pale Raw Sienna in some of the white parts of the clouds in the distance will add a finishing touch to the sky, and a simple landscape of rolling hills can be added with a mixture of Cobalt Blue and Raw Sienna with perhaps a little Burnt Umber in the immediate foreground. As said before, your result will not be exactly like mine, but it should look like the same kind of sky.

Landscape

It might be as well to get in some practice with a single tree before going on to the landscape. Trees are favourites with us all though not always the easiest things to paint. Even the bleakest moor will contain a tree or trees of some kind, even if only wind-bitten thorns, and these can be so interesting to paint in line and shape, often more so than some of the more sedate types. The character of individual trees must be studied and this can be done in depth, by drawing them constantly, either using pencil and pen to describe the linear shapes of branches and trunks in winter, or in charcoal for describing them in mass in summer. When painting a mass of trees, show how the light edges of one tree will show up against a darker neighbour. It is in describing the tonal values, one against the other, which will make the painting read, but keep background trees simple in shape and subdued in colour and tone. When drawing particular trees look to see if the branches grow upwards or bend downwards, or are spreading. Willows are individuals and need special study. Too many students paint them to a formula, without looking and seeing how they really grow. When knowledge of different trees has been gained, don't draw too much in before painting. Let the brush do the work and remember to use the side of the brush. Look for different greens and other colours besides, also for varied colours in the trunks, such as greys and mauves, and not only brown. Notice that individual leaves near the foreground will show reflected light from the sky on top, and so appear bluer. The same leaves will be warmer in colour underneath, ie contain more yellow or red, reflecting the ground. Sometimes students paint trees as though they are going to take off with nothing to hold them to the ground, while others make them look like tree-ferns because the trunk begins to slope too far up the tree. Generally speaking, the branches of young trees grow up towards the light. Later, those growing below spread horizontally in order to seek the light. Summer trees are best painted foliage first particularly in watercolour, with the half-seen branches and trunk added afterwards.

Summer trees can be done in three stages. The shape of the tree is first dropped in with the lightest colour. The next tone is added while the first wash is still slightly damp, and lastly the darks are added. When this is dry,

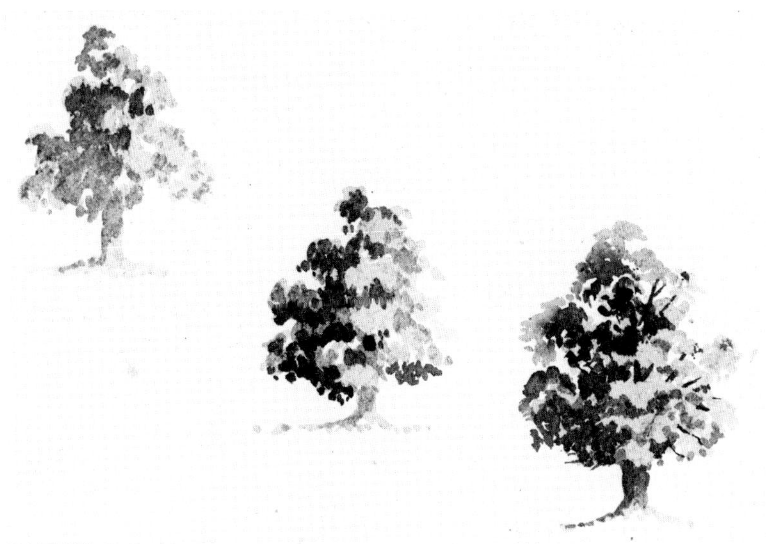

Figure 33   The three stages of painting a tree

the trunk and branches can be added. Remember that trees are round and so the direction of light must be shown, and some of the foliage must be shown lying across the front of the tree. Figure 33 shows the three stages of painting.

For the picture shown in Figure 37, the steps are worked in four stages, and the palette used is Cobalt Blue, Raw Sienna, Olive Green and Light Red. This time, instead of drawing in with a pencil, which can be inhibiting, mix a very pale Cobalt, and draw in with a small brush, the position of the far distance, the trees, the banks and the reeds. The blue drawing, providing it is pale enough, will disappear as the painting progresses. This stage is shown in Figure 34.

The next stage is to paint the sky, leaving the cloud forms for the moment. Drop some blue into the water area while the paper is still damp, but leave white paper for the foreground area of water. Go back to the sky, drop in any other colours necessary and the shadow sides of the clouds, and any darker clouds there may be. Do not keep altering the sky to match the ever-changing one in front of you. Decide on an interpretation, paint it boldly, and *leave it*. The three skies shown in the illustrations were painted one after another from the skies passing in front of me and so all are different because the clouds were moving fast. Figure 35 shows the second stage of painting.

By this time, the middle distance and foreground are dry enough to work on. Remembering the aerial perspective, mix Cobalt Blue and Olive Green and drop in the trees, darkening and adding more green into the nearer

43

Figure 34 Stage one for painting Figure 37

Figure 35 Stage two

44

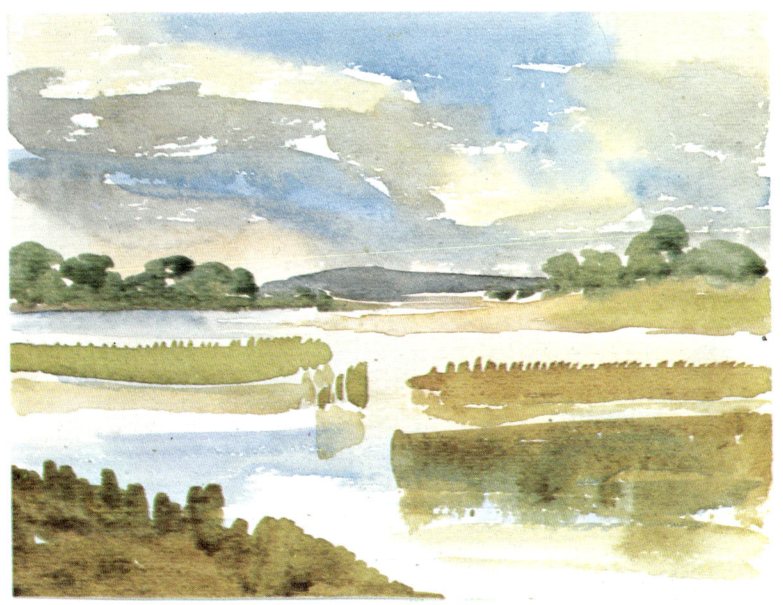

Figure 36 Stage three

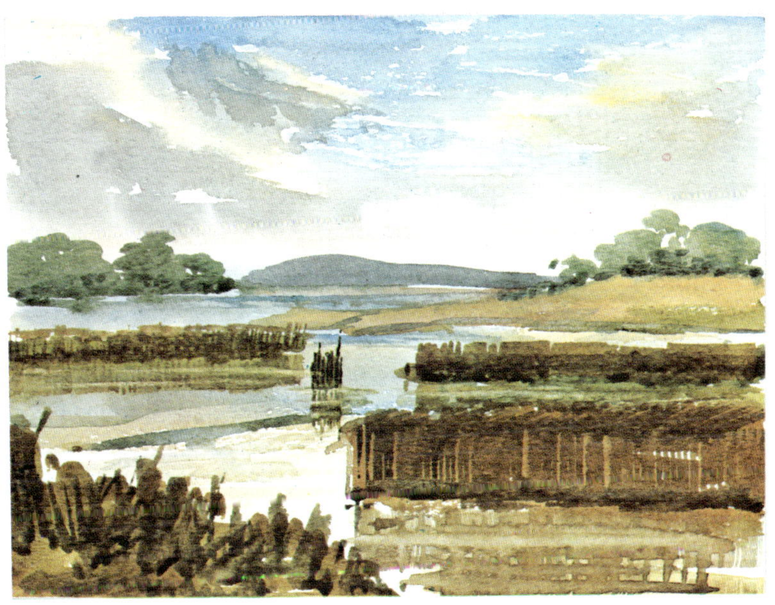

Figure 37 Completed picture

45

ones. Next drop in the reed beds, again remembering the aerial perspective. This stage is shown in Figure 36.

In the last stage, add the finishing touches, such as the darks at the base of the reeds and trees, a few darker streaks in the foreground water, and the reflections. The reeds have been put in with a flat brush, held vertically. The final picture is seen in Figure 37.

The picture, then, has been worked from light to dark, holding on to the lights as long as possible. Two points to remember with reflections are, to keep them directly underneath the thing being reflected, and to remember the perspective of any ripples there may be in the water, the distance between them getting less as they go farther away. If there are no ripples and the water is completely still, the reflection will be a mirror image of the subject. If there are fine grasses in the foreground, it is not always possible to leave them as white paper, in which case, masking fluid can be used to paint them with. This is a rubber solution which, when the painting is finished and completely dry, can be lightly rubbed off, leaving the exposed white paper. Another method which is often used on hand-made paper is to flick out the grasses or masts or whatever it is, with a sharp pen-knife or razor blade.

Still-life and flowers

Still-life

Still-life in watercolour is rather more difficult than landscape because 'happy accidents' cannot be used quite as readily. So, to begin with, choose something simple. Fruit, vegetables and pots of various kinds lend themselves very well and rich, strong colour can be used, either mixed or superimposed. For this exercise, return to the pencil for drawing in, as the shapes must be right before applying the paint. When really experienced in drawing the pencil can be dispensed with and the whole painting done in 'brush drawing', the kind of approach one sees in the paintings of the Chinese and Japanese. For the moment, however, draw carefully but *lightly*, with a soft pencil and without erasing. This is particularly important on Bockingford paper as it is very tender and any disturbance of it will show through the painting.

A still-life is shown in Figure 38, but it is better to set up a similar one of your own than to copy this. The colour of the cloth was obtained by laying it in with Winsor Green, letting it dry, and then superimposing Prussian Blue, which gives more luminosity than mixing the two colours together. Try this with reds, by laying in with one red and superimposing with another. However, this is where it is useful to know which colours are transparent and which opaque. It is better to lay in with a Cadmium Red or a Light Red, both of which are opaque, and to superimpose with Crimson Alizarin or Permanent Rose, both of which are transparent. Although superimposing has its uses, do not try it too much or with too many layers of watercolour, or the painting will become impossibly muddy; use discretion.

Flowers

This technique is particularly useful in the portrayal of flowers. Unlike oil and pastel, sometimes the exact colour for a flower is difficult to achieve in watercolour except by superimposing. In Figure 39 the first square shows French Ultramarine superimposed on Crimson Alizarin, both of which are transparent colours. In the second square the two colours have been mixed together and I hope the printing will show that the first has more depth and

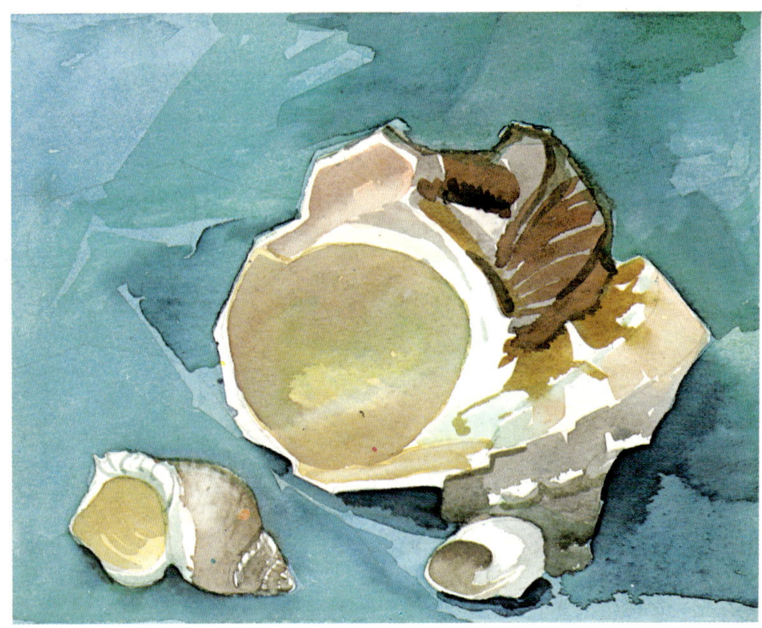

Figure 38   Still-life; background colour is superimposed

is nearer to the colour of a purple anemone than the second. Extra colours
will be needed in the palette for flower painting and the following list will
be useful: Coeruleum Blue, Permanent Rose, Permanent Magenta,
Permanent Violet, Cadmium Red, Scarlet Lake, Cadmium Orange, Aureolin
and Brown Madder Alizarin. All of these colours, particularly the last
named are also useful in landscape and still-life, but do not make the
mistake of using too many colours at once in the same painting.

Students often ask whether backgrounds should be put into flower
paintings and, if so, should they go in first or last. Personally, I feel that

Figure 39   The first sequence has been superimposed; the second is mixed

48

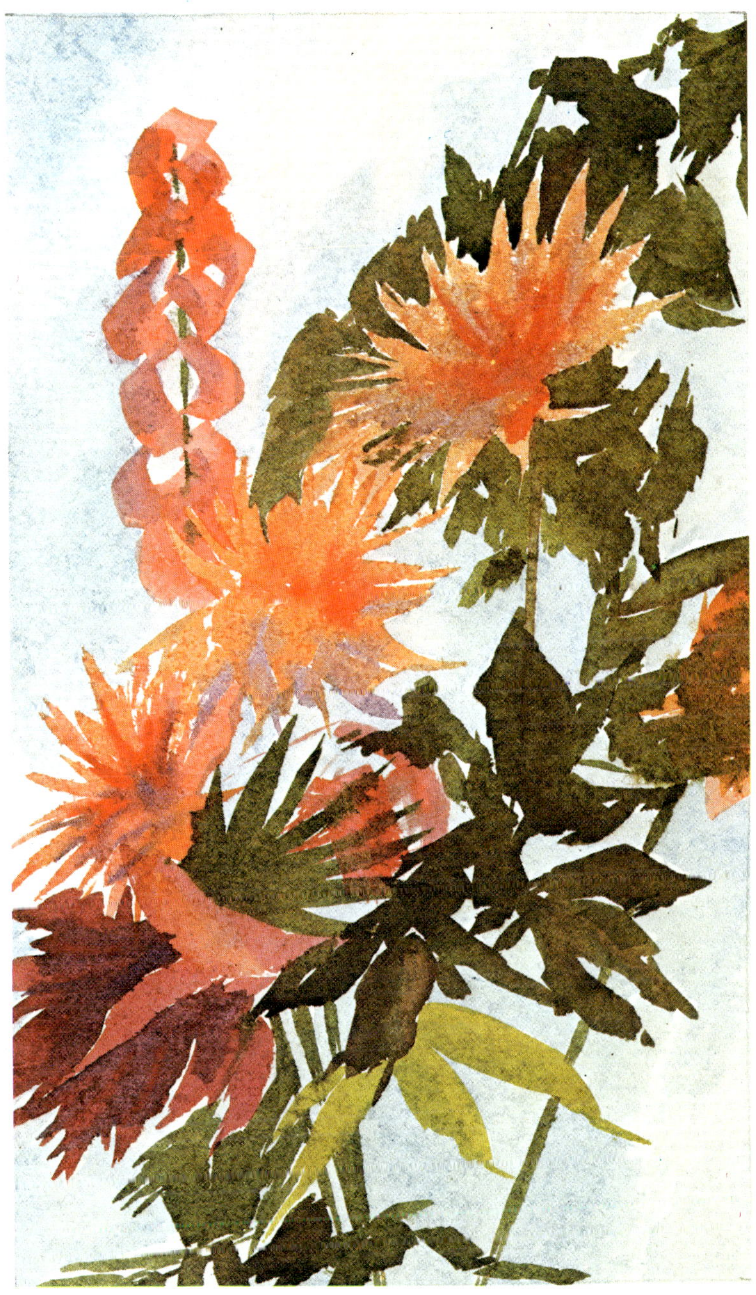

Figure 40   Flowers; background put in last

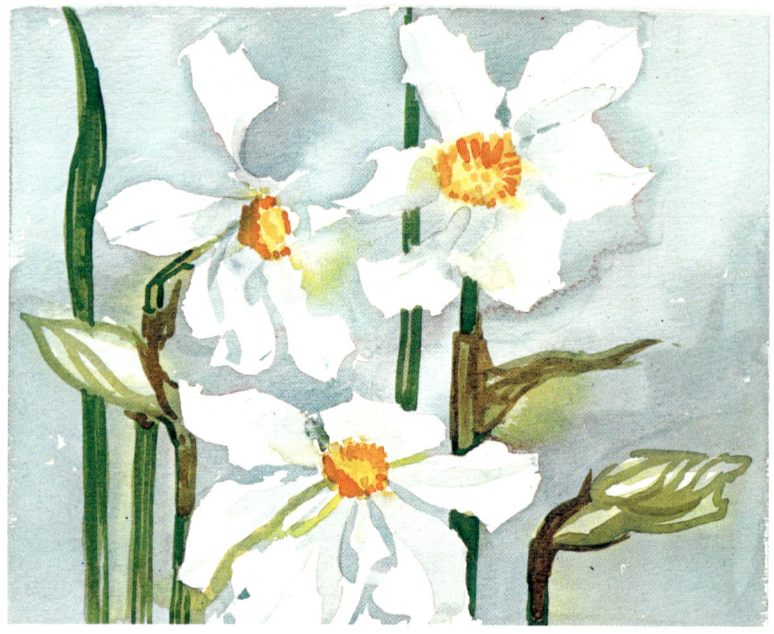

Figure 41   White flowers; paper left for whites so background is put in first

backgrounds should be put in, otherwise the painting becomes a study. Botanical, highly detailed, flower studies rarely have backgrounds, and delightful as they are, are not really pictures as such, and what is more, need very specialized study and talents. If this kind of flower painting appeals to you, courses dealing specifically with this method are often run.

For picture-making, backgrounds should be put in and can go in either first or last, or as the painting proceeds which is a bit more difficult. The easiest way is to put it in last. Having painted the flowers, leaves and pot, if any, wet the paper that is left, right up to the painted areas. Have the background colour ready mixed, and sufficient of it. It need not necessarily be all the same colour or tone, but if it is going to be a variegated wash, have all the colours and tones to be used, mixed ready. When the shine has gone off the paper, beginning at the top, let the wash or washes run down the paper, guiding into the detailed areas, but not taking it quite up to the painted edges. The dampish paper will carry the colour just to where it is needed and no farther, but will combine happily with them, as in Figure 40. White flowers, of course, must be left as white paper but must not appear too hard and 'cut-out'. Again, the secret is to paint them on slightly damp paper, putting in the background round them and sharpening up any necessary edges afterwards, as in Figure 41.

50

Gouache and acrylics

Gouache

Gouache has been mentioned earlier as being an opaque, water-based medium. It is included nowadays in the exhibitions of the Royal Institute of Watercolour Painters.

The medium is sold in tubes marked as Designer's Gouache. Pots of poster paint have the same effect and are cheaper, but probably not so permanent or finely ground. The one disadvantage the Designer's Gouache has, is that it dries up in the tubes. However, if a little water is put into the top of the tube, after using, and before screwing down the cap tightly, this will solve the problem. To ensure permanence it is a good idea, when

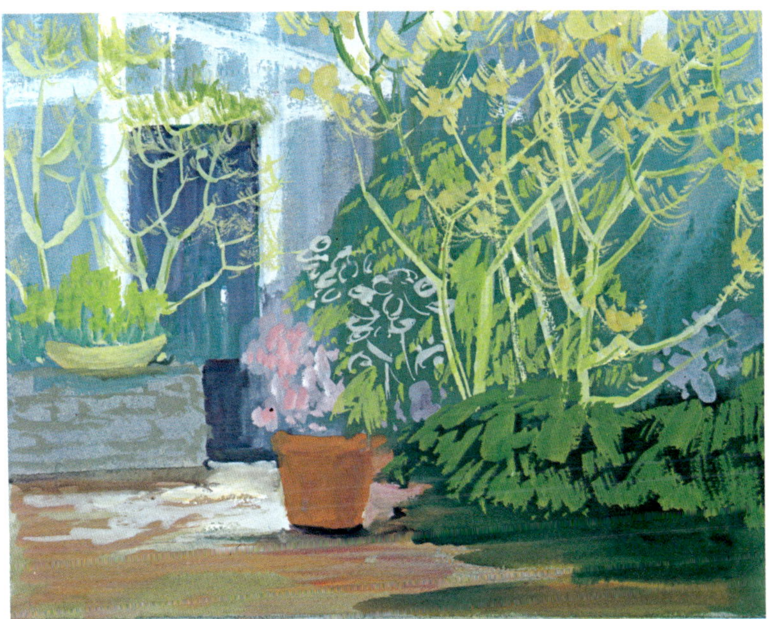

Figure 42 Using gouache on grey paper

buying gouache, to purchase the approximate colours to the watercolour palette. Sometimes the names are different but the catalogue will state which colours are permanent.

It may be thought that it is an easier medium than watercolour and in some ways it is, but it is still quite a tricky medium, partly because there are so many ways of handling it. Watercolourists who try it for the first time find it confusing because it is more akin to oil painting, where white must be used as a pigment and not the paper itself. However, it has an attractive, elusive quality and can be very effective in misty scenes or in 'lost and found' effects, and has a pearly, matt finish which is very pleasing. This medium suits a more creative type of painting rather than straight-forward interpretations of nature, and beautiful effects can be obtained by painting fairly thinly on tinted paper. Used with Aquapasto, a vehicle bought in a tube from the art shop, gouache is excellent for knife-painting on paper. The Aquapasto is necessary so that the thick layer of gouache will not crack, and the gouache can be thinned down a little with water, as can the Aquapasto.

Figure 42 is painted with water only on a Turner Grey paper and the colours used are Permanent White, Cadmium Yellow, Crimson Alizarin, French Ultramarine and Raw Umber.

Acrylics

Acrylic paint has been around for some time now and many professional painters use it exclusively. It is a water-based medium and should not be confused with Alkyd, which has recently been introduced into the fine arts market, as this is an oil-based paint. Like gouache, it needs getting used to, but unlike gouache, once a wash or layer of acrylic paint is laid down, it is immovable, so it is not so easy to get the diffuse, melting quality of gouache. Although it is water-based, it sets very quickly so brushes must be kept in water during each painting session and washed very thoroughly in weak detergent at the end. One of the great advantages of this medium is that any support can be used. Papers of all kinds, including newspaper, wood, hardboard, cardboard, metal, canvas, and even brick and stone can all be used, either with an acrylic primer or without. It can be used in a manner similar to that of oil, gouache or watercolour, but has properties peculiar to itself, which perhaps suggest the best way in which to use it. As it dries so quickly, it lends itself to being built up in glazes. Unlike oil, there is little or no waiting time between each glaze and it can be built up to great brilliance and luminosity. If used in a manner appertaining to watercolour it is accepted in the exhibitions of the Royal Institute of Watercolour Painters. Different acrylic mediums and glazes can be bought for different effects but it can be used quite satisfactorily with water only. Other mediums can be painted over it, but it will peel off if put on the top of another medium, other than watercolour. Keep finished pictures separated in storage because they are inclined to stick to anything in juxtaposition. Because of its adhesive qualities, it is best to use a glass, enamel, or laminated plastic palette. Any kind of brushes may be used.

Preservation

Storing

Storing watercolours is much easier and less space-consuming than either pastels or oil paintings. Either keep them flat in a drawer, or in a portfolio, preferably laid flat. Portfolios are not difficult to make. Two stout pieces of cardboard, fastened together at the base with masking or adhesive fabric tape and kept together with a large bull-dog clip at the top will serve very well. If there is insufficient space to lay them flat, place the paintings in a large plastic bag inside the portfolio, so that they do not slide and curve at the base. The most important thing to guard against is storing them in a damp place. Try to keep them, and the watercolour paper, in the driest part of the house because if they get damp, mould marks will appear in due course and spoil them.

Mounting and framing

If the paintings are going to be framed, they will need a mount, glass and a backing. Turn screws are useful for fastening the lot into the frame, as they can be turned to allow pictures to be changed easily when required. A reasonably wide mount sets off a painting and even if it is not going to be framed immediately, it should never be shown without a mount. It is surprising how a watercolour is enhanced by its mount. Although they are expensive, unless one is an expert at cutting them it is best left to the professional, as a tatty mount can spoil a good picture. However, it can be done with a sharp-bladed modelling knife and a piece of angled metal, obtainable from a do-it-yourself shop. There is also on the market a Dexter Mount Cutter, which I understand is very efficient and might be worth investing in, if a lot of mounts have to be cut. For a picture about 50 × 48 cm (20 × 19 in) a mount needs to be 65 mm (2½ in) wide at the top and sides and 75 mm (3 in) wide at the bottom. Sometimes, the smaller the picture, the larger the mount can be in relation to it. Generally the safest colour is an ivory, but not a cream or a brilliant white. For certain pictures, dark mounts are attractive, but it is very much a matter of personal taste. If you wish to sell your pictures, an ivory mount is the one most likely to go with people's decor, which, whether we like it or not, needs to be thought

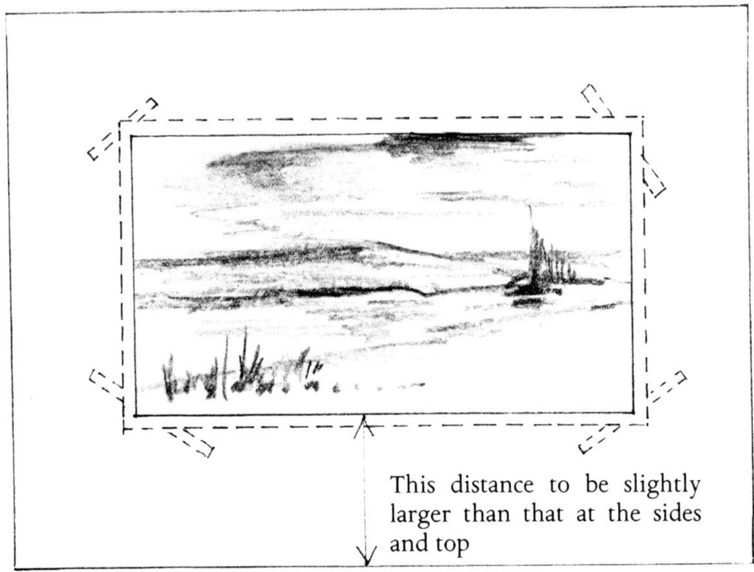

Figure 43   How mount fits over the picture

about. They are also more likely to be selected for exhibitions, all else being equal, because dark mounts are sometimes difficult to hang with other pictures. To cut a mount use a sharp, craft knife with expendable blades and angled metal. Place the mounting card on a large board and/or a thick pad of newspapers. Cut the outside edge to fit the glassed area of the frame. Measure carefully and mark very lightly the area of the picture required to show, letting the margin of mount be a little wider at the bottom than it is at the top and sides; Figure 43 explains the measurements. Holding the metal angle against the side that needs cutting, cut steadily and slowly at a slight angle so that the cut is bevelled. Be particularly careful at the corners, so that the knife does not shoot over the edge and cut into the mount where it is not wanted. When the four sides are cut, remove the centre from the mount. Place the picture to be mounted on a cleared table, place the mount on top, and bring the two together to the edge of the table and fasten a piece of transparent adhesive tape across the corner of the mount and the picture underneath. Repeat this for each corner, and then turn the whole thing over and fasten properly with transparent adhesive tape along each edge. Place in frame and fix the hardboard backing in, either with turn screws or panel pins and seal with wide masking tape. 'D' rings or eyelets should be fastened about a third of the way down on the back, but be careful not to drill right through the moulding. Simple frames are the best for watercolours, not too narrow, with perhaps a gold line in the moulding and preferably a light colour tying up with something in the picture. Natural oak is attractive, and tough but it does discolour with age. Another possibility is to make the frame from kits which are not difficult to put together but a clamp may be needed to hold the corners, during assembly. The kits are much cheaper than ready made frames which are very expensive indeed.

Watercolour with other media

Charcoal

Before talking about combining watercolour with charcoal, I should like to make an appreciative acknowledgement to Edward Swann, who was not only an organizer of painting holidays for over thirty years and gave enormous pleasure to countless numbers of people, but was also an inspired and enthusiastic teacher, particularly with beginners. Using charcoal in the following manner was his inspired idea to show beginners the importance of tonal values in painting. In fact he called it 'charcoal painting' and it is quite a different approach from charcoal drawing. Many examples of this method will be shown in his book called *Prelude to Painting Improvement*, published by Charles Skilton Ltd (1974). A good, thick cartridge paper should be used for this, rather than watercolour paper which may give a grainy look to the picture and detract from the tonal qualities. *Gently* stroke the *point* of a piece of medium willow charcoal over the paper, from side to side and from top to bottom. There should be a layer of paper underneath the top sheet so that the grain of the board will not be taken up when the charcoal is passed across. Do not use the side of the charcoal but be careful not to dig the point into the paper or lines may be left which will be difficult to eradicate. Should the charcoal be at all scratchy or brownish change it at once for another piece. When the paper has been covered, rub the charcoal in gently with the fingers, tissue or cotton wool until an even, half-tone surface is produced. In Figure 44 will be seen one half of the paper with the charcoal laid in and the other half showing it rubbed to an even half-tone. For the next stage, shown in Figure 45, a putty or kneaded rubber will be part of the equipment. Not, I hasten to add, to correct mistakes, but to *draw* the lights, by lifting out the charcoal. Break off about a quarter of the rubber for use and, as its name implies, it can be kneaded into a point, or a thin line or anything that may be necessary. Having taken out the main lights with the rubber, accentuate the main darks with the charcoal. In the third stage, Figure 46 shows these two processes taken to a conclusion with the details, and what Edward called the 'half-crown' touches added (for those of you who remember what that was). When finished, prop the painting up and spray it with fixative either with a mouth-spray or an

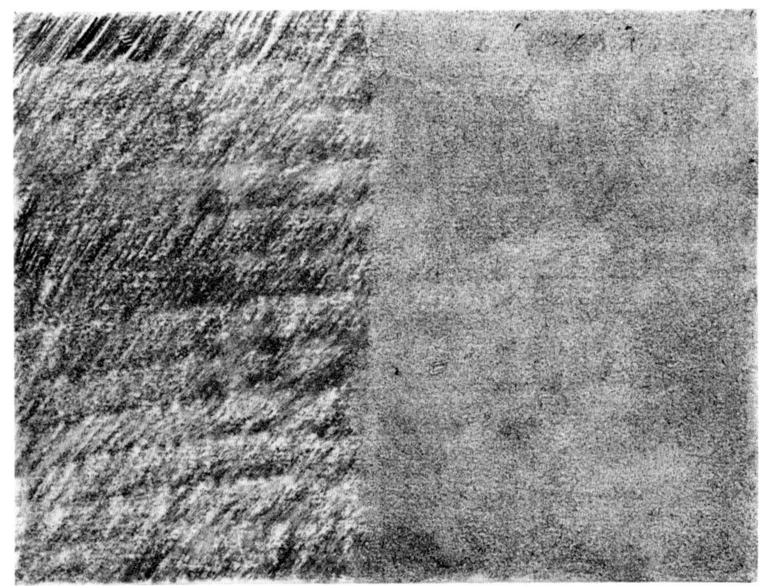

Figure 44 Stage one; charcoal unrubbed and charcoal rubbed

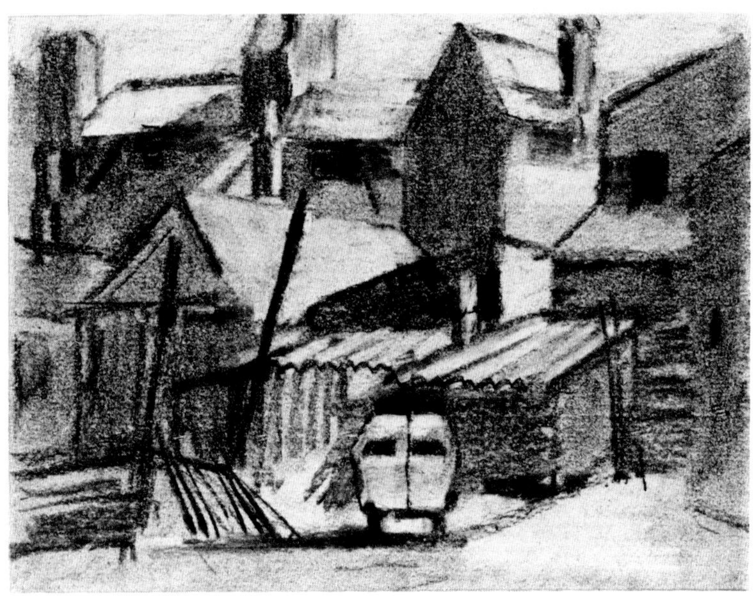

Figure 45 Stage two; main lights and darks established

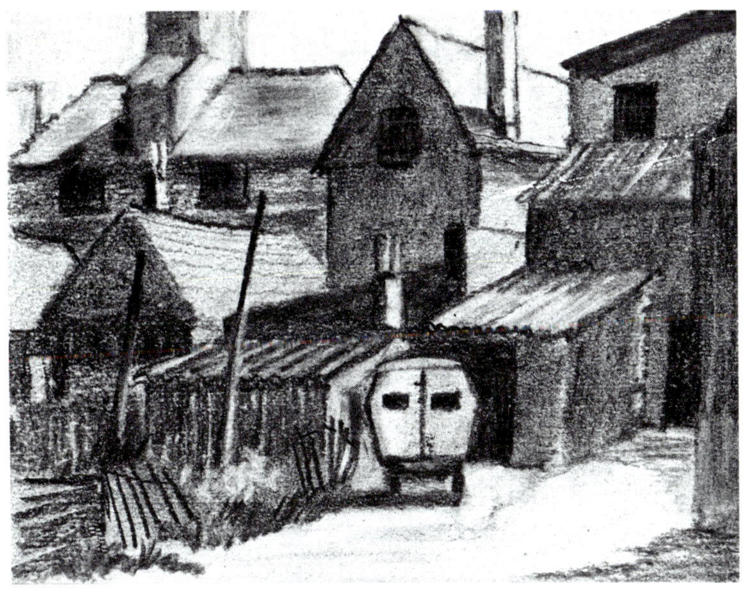

Figure 46   Stage three; charcoal brought to a conclusion

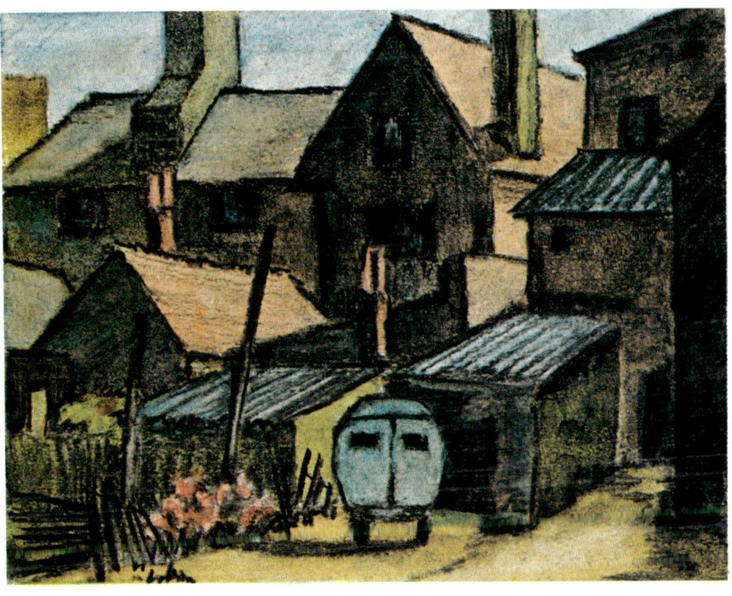

Figure 47   Stage four; wash put over charcoal after fixing

aerosol. Hold it about 30 cm (12 in) away from the paper and pass across it from top to bottom and allow it to dry, which will only take a few minutes. Test it with a finger to make quite sure that it is fixed, otherwise it will smear into the watercolour when it is applied. Give it another spray if necessary. When the paper is completely dry, float the watercolour over in transparent washes, in the appropriate colours, being sure to keep them very transparent so that the tonal work with the charcoal can shine through, and you should be pleased with the result. Figure 47 shows a finished charcoal with watercolour.

Line and wash

A good way of beginning the difficult art of watercolour painting is to start with line-and-wash as the line gives something to lean on before the watercolour technique is established. For experienced painters the line can go in first or last, according to choice, but the easiest way to learn, is to put the line first and lean on it quite heavily for shadows and textures. The support should be one of the watercolour papers but the drawing tools can be various, according to taste. Some people like a drawing pen, using a Waverley type nib, or a relief nib which will give thick and thin strokes. Never use a mapping pen, which can be frustrating in the extreme. If your choice is for a fine, even line use a Rotring pen which has interchangeable tops of different thicknesses. Others like to use a fine brush and the finer Chinese brushes are particularly good for this and are obtainable at good art shops. Various fibre-tip pens can be used but be sure that the ink is not the soluble kind, which will run when the watercolour is put on. This kind of soluble fibre-tip can be useful as a sketching tool, as the drawing can be done with the pen and then clear water brushed over with a small brush to give the tones – not much to carry! An example of this can be seen in Figure 48. Felt pens can be used if working on a large scale but for normal size work they are rather gross. Pencils of all kinds can give a good strong line and the best of these include soft graphite, carbon pencils, Conté pencils and Conté crayons. Charcoal pencils I have never found very satisfactory, preferring to use the stick charcoal which can be rubbed to a sharp point if wanted. However, a favourite tool of many artists, and of mine, is a sharpened matchstick fastened to a penholder, or even just a sharpened piece of wood or bamboo. The best ink to use is waterproof Indian ink, except in the case of the Rotring pen which has its own ink.

Figure 49 shows a painting where the line has been put in first with a fine Chinese brush and waterproof Indian ink, and then the colour has been added in simple washes.

If the line is added afterwards as in Figure 50, using a Rotring pen with ·35 and ·5 nibs, this gives more freedom to the washes, and less line is used, as the shadows are usually put in with the colour rather than the Indian ink, but, as in so many aspects of painting, there is no hard and fast rule and personal choice takes preference.

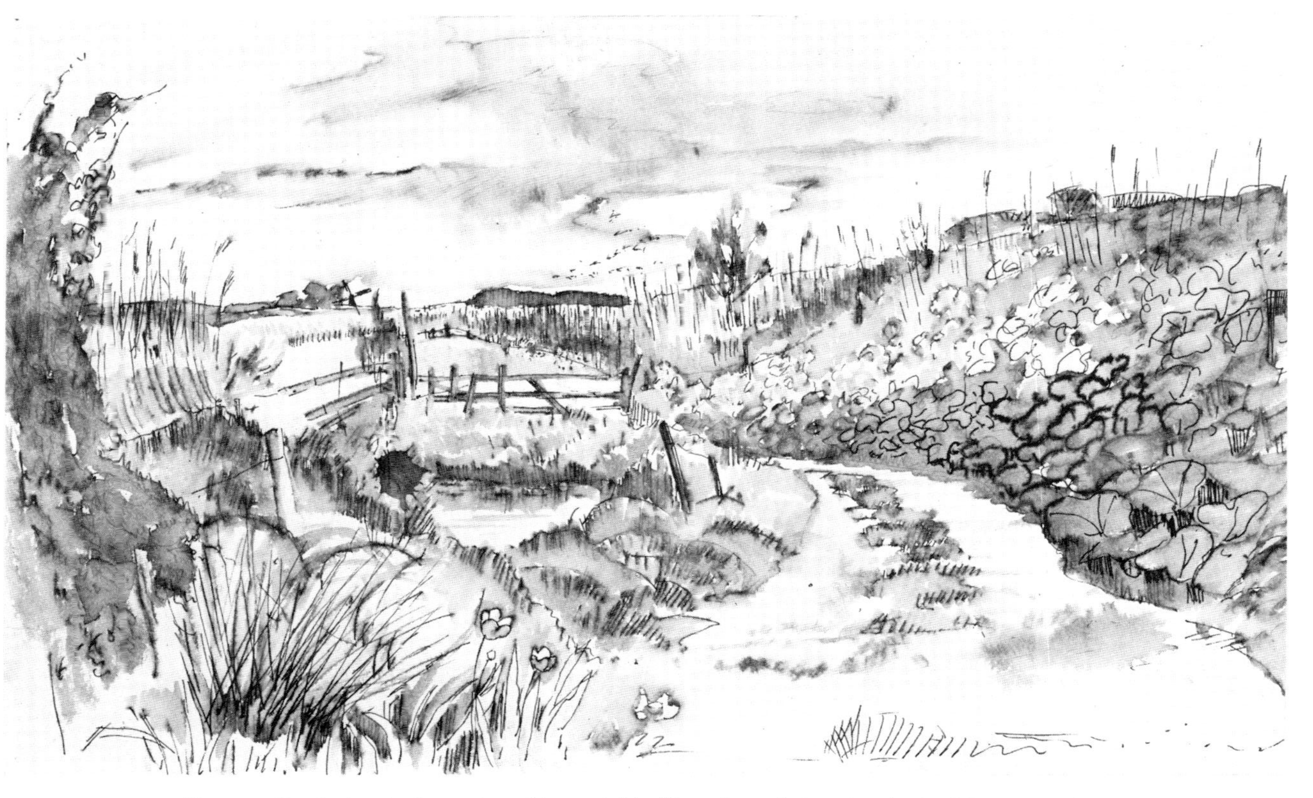

Figure 48   A sketch drawn in with a soluble fibre tip and then brushed with water only

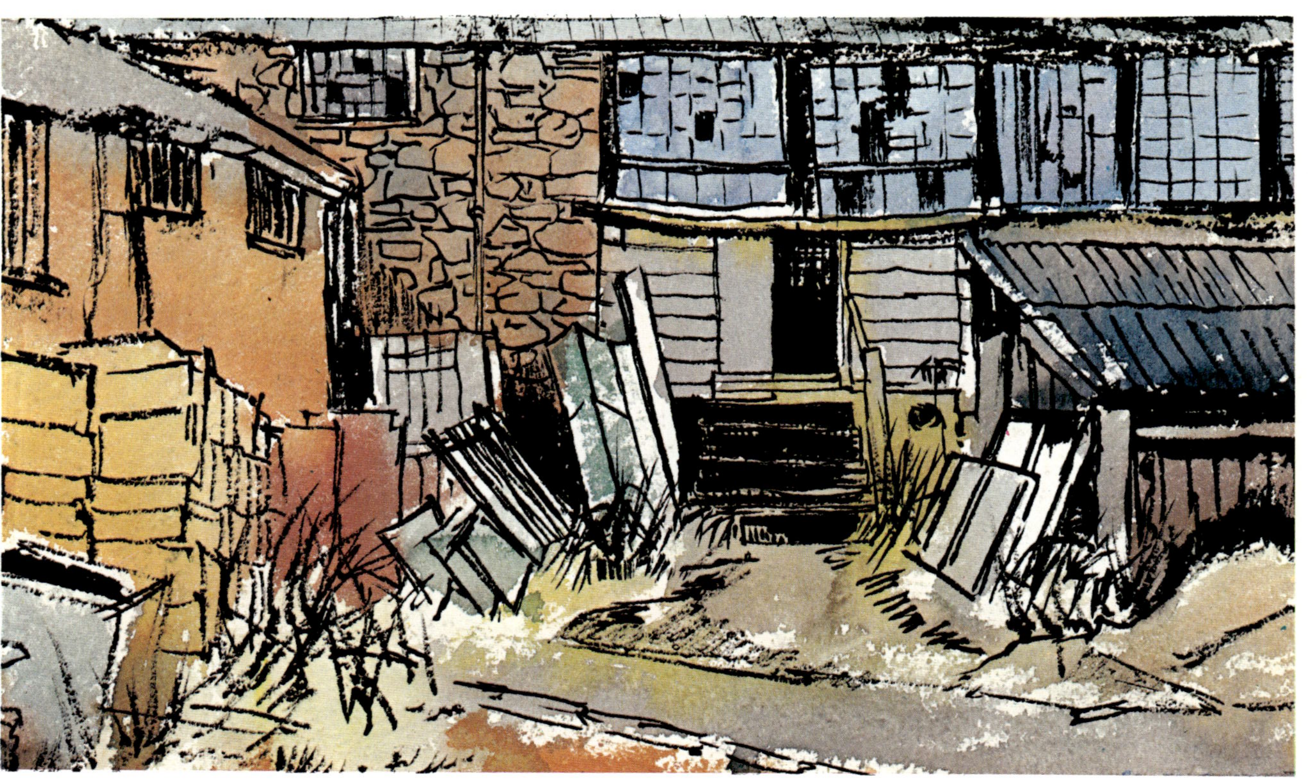

Figure 49 Line put in first with a fine Chinese brush and Indian ink; the line varies in thickness

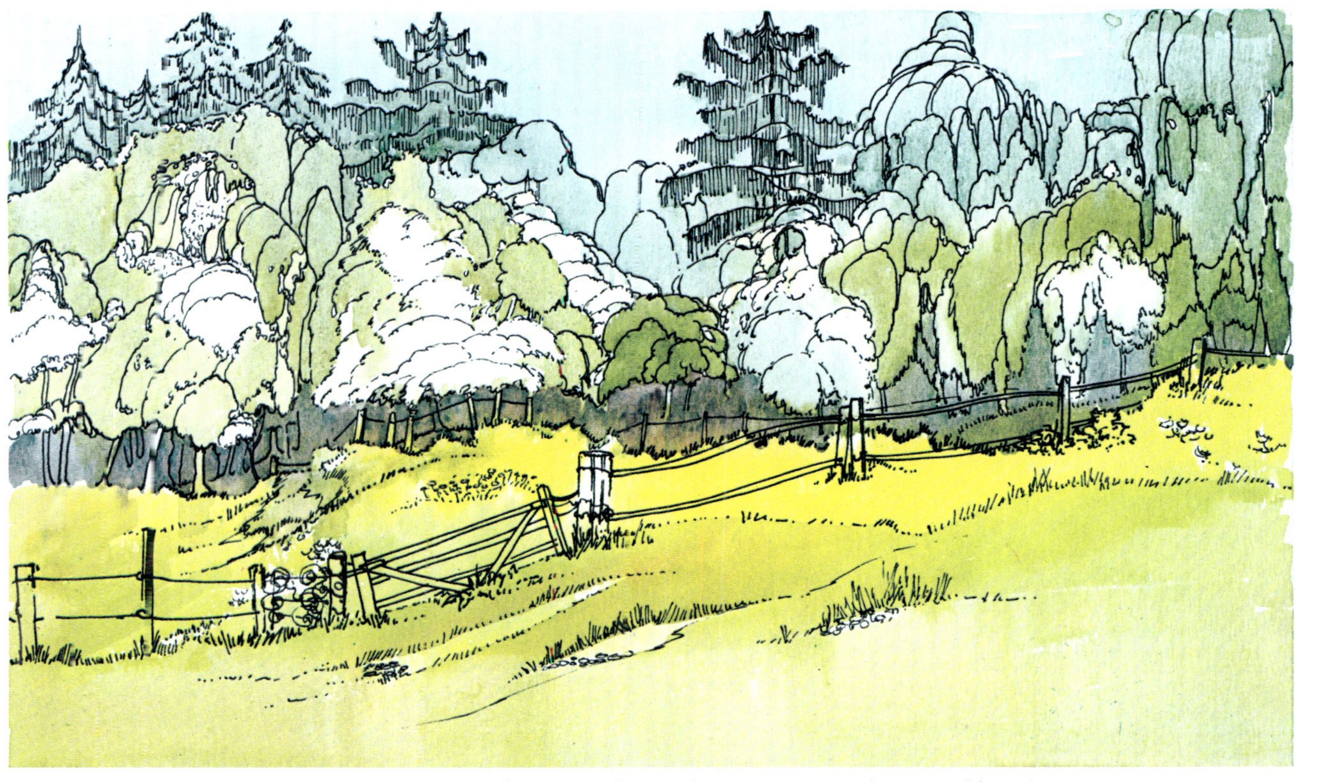

Figure 50   Line put in after watercolour with a Rotring pen, nib size 5. Although the line is the same throughout, it can be varied by changing the nib

Pastel

Pastel can often pull a failed watercolour together, though I do not really advocate this. It can also be used with a purpose, either to enhance a very loose wash, in order to give some 'bones', or pastel can be used first, fixed well and then have watercolour washed over it.

Summing up

To sum up, it is useful to remember six points in particular when painting in watercolour:
1 Have sufficient mixture of paint ready
2 Keep the paint well stirred
3 Work always with a full brush
4 Keep the paint flowing but under control
5 Never let the brush go over any part twice during one process
6 Be prepared to begin again

One of the most important things to remember when painting in any medium is to keep looking and really observing. Never be without a sketch-book, and keep drawing.